CHUMS IN DIXIE

OR, THE STRANGE CRUISE OF A MOTORBOAT

ST. GEORGE RATHBORNE

1st WORLD
LIBRARY
Literary Society

Chums in Dixie

St. George Rathborne

© 1st World Library, 2009
PO Box 2211
Fairfield, IA 52556
www.1stworldlibrary.com
First Edition

LCCN: 2009923391

Softcover ISBN: 978-1-4218-8836-1
Hardcover ISBN: 978-1-4218-8935-1
eBook ISBN: 978-1-4218-8737-1

Purchase *"Chums in Dixie"*
as a traditional bound book at:
www.1stWorldLibrary.com/purchase.asp?ISBN=978-1-4218-8836-1

1st World Library is a literary, educational organization
dedicated to:

- Creating a free internet library of downloadable ebooks

- Hosting writing competitions and offering book publishing
  scholarships.

Interested in more 1st World Library books? contact:
literacy@1stworldlibrary.com
Check us out at: www.1stworldlibrary.com

1ˢᵗ World Library Literary Society

Giving Back to the World

"If you want to work on the core problem, it's early school literacy."

- James Barksdale, former CEO of Netscape

"No skill is more crucial to the future of a child, or to a democratic and prosperous society, than literacy."

- Los Angeles Times

"Literacy... means far more than learning how to read and write... The aim is to transmit... knowledge and promote social participation."

- UNESCO

"Literacy is not a luxury, it is a right and a responsibility. If our world is to meet the challenges of the twenty-first century we must harness the energy and creativity of all our citizens."

- President Bill Clinton

"Parents should be encouraged to read to their children, and teachers should be equipped with all available techniques for teaching literacy, so the varying needs and capacities of individual kids can be taken into account."

- Hugh Mackay

CONTENTS

CHAPTER I

THE VOYAGE BEGUN

"Phil, oh! Phil, won't you please hurry up? I'll go to sleep pretty soon, if we don't get a move on us."

"Just give me five minutes more, Larry, and I promise you we're going to leave this place, and start on our cruise down to the big Gulf. I've got a couple of nuts to put on again, and then you'll hear the little motor begin to hum."

The last speaker was bending over the engine of a fair-sized motor boat, which had a stationary roof, and adjustable curtains that in time of need could be made to enclose the entire vessel.

This modern craft was tied up against the bank of one of those narrow but swift streams that, having their source in southern Georgia or Alabama, find their way to the Gulf of Mexico, after passing through many miles of Florida cypress swamps that are next to unknown territory to the outside world.

Phil Lancing was the son of a well-to-do Northern physician, who had some time previously come into possession of a very large tract of territory in Northern Florida. Considerable of this property was in vast swamps; and here squatters had settled many years back, cutting the trees at their pleasure, and making vast quantities of cypress shingles, which were floated down the river to markets along the gulf.

The second occupant of the brave launch Aurora was a rather chubby specimen of a half grown lad, with a rosy face, and laughing blue eyes. Larry Densmore expected to become a lawyer some fine day, and in evidence of his fitness for the business he was constantly asking questions, and finding debatable points in such matters as naturally came up.

Phil being an amateur naturalist, knew considerable about the woods and their numerous denizens. Larry was an utter greenhorn, and apt many times to display his gross ignorance concerning the habits of game; as well as the thousand and one things a woodsman is supposed to be acquainted with. But his good-nature was really without limit; and one could hardly ever get provoked with Larry, even when he committed the most stupendous of blunders.

Upon hearing these consoling words from his chum, Larry, who was sitting well up in the bow of the boat, yawned and stretched himself. The southern sun was inclined to be warm, and Larry had not slept very well the two nights he had been aboard the motor boat. But then it was nothing very singular to see the chubby lad yawning at any time of the day.

"I'm real glad we've got all our supplies aboard," he said, aloud, just to pass the time away, and to keep awake while Phil was fussing with the engine preparatory to starting on their trip down-stream. "I'm tired of this dead little village that they call a town. And tired of hearing what an awful lot of trouble we're bound to buck up against when we get two-thirds of the way down to the gulf. Wonder what they'd say if they knew your dad owned most all of that property along this crazy old creek they call a river. And that you even expect to stop off to interview that terrible McGee they talk about! Oh, my! what was that, now?"

Larry ceased to stretch himself. He even sat up, his eyes wide open now, as if he had noticed something away out of the usual; and they were fastened on the stern of the boat, where he had certainly seen something slip over the gunwale, and vanish under a pile of blankets that had been airing.

Phil raised his head. He did not even glance at his chum, but seemed to be listening intently.

"Now what d'ye suppose all that shouting means?" he exclaimed. "Seems to be coming this way too, and mighty fast at that. There, look, Larry, don't you see them running through the woods? As sure as you live they're coming this way! I wonder if it's a fox hunt, or what?"

"Mebbe—" began Larry; and then his comrade interrupted him before he could say what was on his mind.

"They're heading right for us; and there's that big Colonel Brashears at their head, the fellow who told us all those awful stories about the shingle-makers of the swamps. Here they come, seven of 'em; and look, Larry, as many as four have got ugly whips in their hands! Something's up, I tell you."

Again did Larry open his mouth as though to say something; and for the second time, after a swift glance toward the blankets, he closed it again resolutely.

The seven men who were running speedily drew near. Most of them were out of breath, and all looked very much excited. The leader, who was quite a character in the Southern town, and a fierce appearing individual, with a military swagger, which Phil believed to be wholly assumed, immediately addressed himself to the two young Northerners on the new-fangled motor boat, which had been the wonder of the townspeople ever since it was dropped off the cars to be launched in the so-called "river" at their doors.

"Seen anything of him acomin' this aways, sah?" he asked, in a high pitched, raspy voice. "We done chased him through the woods, and he's give us the slip. Thinkin' he mout have come in this direction, we changed our course to put the question to yuh."

"What was it—a fox?" asked Phil, innocently enough.

"No, sah, it was not a fox, but a miserable whelp of a boy!" exclaimed the indignant colonel, drawing his military figure up, and cracking his whip with a vindictive report that sounded like the discharge of a pistol.

"A boy?" ejaculated Phil, astonished at all this display of force under such peculiar conditions.

"A boy!" echoed Larry, some of the color leaving his face, and a look of genuine concern taking its place.

"A mighty sassy and desp'rit critter at that," the colonel went on. "One of that McGee tribe from down-river way. He's been loafin' 'round town some days, I'm told, an' we're lucky not to have our homes robbed o' everything wuth while. My Bob met him on the street a while back; an' jest like boys, they had words that led to blows. The miserable beggar actually had the nerve to lick my Bob; foh yuh see I reckon he's just like a wildcat in a fight. When I seen the black eye and bloody nose he give my Bob I jest natchally ached to lay it on him; and organizin' a posse o' my neighbors, who has reason to hate them McGees like cold pizen, we started out to lay hands on the cub an' tan his hide black an' blue."

"But he managed to escape after all, you say?" asked Phil, who had some difficulty in keeping a grin of satisfaction from showing on his face; for the idea of these seven stalwart men chasing one puny little chap was pretty close to ridiculous in his eyes.

"He was too slick foh us, I reckons, sah," the colonel went on, snapping off the heads of a few wild flowers with the lash of his constantly moving whip. "We done lost sight of him in the woods, and thought as how possibly you mout aseen him thisaways. And so we turned aside to ask you that question, sah."

Phil shook his head in the negative.

"I give you my word, Colonel Brashears, I haven't seen the least sign of any boy for the last five hours," he said, positively, and with truth. "I've been busy making a few changes in my engine here; and we expect to start down the river inside of five minutes or so."

"Thet's all right, sah," returned the other, with a slight bow. "And such bein' the case me and my posse had better be turnin' our attention in another quarter. We're gwine tuh find that little scamp yet, and tickle his hide foh him. When he goes back tuh his kind below, they'll understand that weuns up-river don't tolerate thieves and brawlers in ouh town. Good day, sah, and we sure hope you-all may have a pleasant voyage; but we done warn yuh tuh look sharp when yuh gets nigh the stampin' place o' the terrible McGee!"

The posse turned away, and went trooping back into the open

woods. Larry had listened to all that was being said with his mouth half open, and a look of real concern on his face. He saw with a thrill that once the leader of the crowd seemed to pause, as if to dispute with his men as to what their next best course might be.

"Oh, do hurry, Phil!" cried the watching lad, as he jumped up from his seat, and going ashore, started to unfasten the cable that held the motor boat to a tree.

"In a minute or two, Chum Larry!" sang out; the other. "What's your haste? Upon my word, I never knew you to act like that before. Generally you're the last one to want to rush things. See here, was it the visit of those fellows that upset you, Larry?"

"Yes, yes," answered the other, with a voice that actually trembled with anxiety; "that Colonel Brashears is such a fierce fire-eater, and he cracked that awful whip just like he itched to lay it on the bare back of that poor little chap. Let's get out of this before they can come back. Why, they might even want to search our boat, you know!"

"Oh! I guess there's no danger of that," laughed Phil. "Anyway, you can see that they've gone into the woods again."

"And headed down-stream; notice that, Phil," went on the stout boy, nervously. "Say, I'm going to unfasten the rope now, and let her swing off on the current. It will give us a start, you know, and make me feel easier."

"All right, let her slip," answered the engineer; "I'm just about ready to turn the engine, and get power on her. Come aboard, Larry. We're off!"

Phil waved his hat, and gave a little cheer as the Aurora began to move through the dark water of the stream, with her nose pointing due south. The merry popping of her unmuffled exhaust told that the engine was busily at work, even if turned on at part speed.

When he saw the shore slipping rapidly by Larry seemed to breathe easier. Still, he kept his gaze fastened upon the woods, as though not quite sure that the posse might not unexpectedly heave in sight again, with a new demand.

For a short time there was silence aboard the rapidly speeding boat. Phil busied himself with his engine, watching its performance with more or less satisfaction; for his heart was set on mechanics, and he anticipated great things of the motor he had put into his boat before sending her south for this especial trip.

Larry on the other hand never once turned to look at the shore along the larboard quarter; that which he knew sheltered the seven burly boy hunters claimed all his attention.

"I wonder will they find the poor little chap?" Phil finally remarked; showing that after all his thoughts were not wholly taken up with the working of the engine at which he was gazing so proudly.

"Say, did you hear what he said about the swamp boy licking his Bob?" demanded Larry, with sudden glee. "Don't you remember what we thought of that big loafer; and how he seemed to lord it over all the other boys of the town, when they came out in a bunch to see what our boat looked like? I'm awful glad he got his, ain't you, Phil?"

"Sure I am," grinned the other. "Thought at one time I'd have to tackle Bob on my own account, when he got so sassy; but

I knew his dad would make it rough for us, and I managed to hold in. Yes, he got only what he deserved, I guess. And if I ever meet up with that swamp boy, I declare I'd like to shake hands with him, and tell him he is all right for doing what he did. It took some nerve to tackle Bob—just like a little rooster going next door and licking the cock of the barnyard."

"Would you really like to tell him that?" exclaimed Larry, as he clutched the shoulder of his chum; and Phil, looking up was astonished to see how his eyes danced.

"Give you my word I would," he declared, vehemently.

"Good!" ejaculated the other, with a nervous laugh; and springing over to a spot nearer the stern of the boat he called out: "You might as well come out now. The colonel and his crowd are far away, and we want to see what you look like!"

Thereupon, to the immense amazement of Phil Lancing, the blankets began to heave; and being speedily tossed aside, behold there came forth the figure of a tattered, half-grown boy—a boy with a face as brown as that of an Indian, and with a pair of defiant black eyes that flashed fire as he looked straight at the owner of the motor boat.

And Phil realized that he was gazing upon the boy belonging to the terrible McGee tribe from down-river, who had just licked the big Brashears cub in his own home town!

St. George Rathborne

CHAPTER II

A BOY OF THE SWAMPS

"Well, if this don't beat all creation!" exclaimed Phil, as he continued to stare at the uninvited passenger on board the Aurora. "See here, Larry, own up now that you saw him crawl aboard our boat?"

"That's just what I did," chuckled the other, as though he enjoyed the joke. "If you hark back a bit, perhaps you'll remember my calling out, just at the time you discovered moving figures through the trees? That was because I had caught just a glimpse of something, I didn't know what, slipping under the blankets.

"Now I can understand why you were so nervous, and wanted to hurry off," said Phil. "You were afraid the fierce colonel would come back, and search our craft for stowaways."

"Sure I was; I admit it," echoed Larry. "But Phil, you really meant what you said just now, didn't you—about wanting to shake hands with the boy who knocked Bob Brashears galley west, you know?"

Phil turned to the sallow-faced, defiant figure that was

observing their every action. The boy looked as though ready to brave them to their face, if so be they turned out to be new enemies; or even take a header over the side, should they show signs of wanting to detain him against his will.

But as soon as he looked into the smiling countenance of Phil he must have realized that in taking this liberty of boarding the motor boat, when so hard pressed by his enemies, he had made a lucky move indeed. For in those friendly eyes he saw genuine warmth.

"Shake hands, won't you, my friend?" said Phil, thrusting out his own digits in the free and easy fashion customary with boys. "I'm glad you punched that Bob Brashears. I hope his black eye will hang to him for a month. And I'd have given a heap to have seen the mill when you licked him. I'm only surprised he dared tackle you alone, big cub that he is."

"Huh!" the boy broke out with, as a glimmer of a smile appeared flickering athwart his thin, serious looking face; "they was two of 'em, mister. But t'other, he run like a scart rabbit the first crack he got under his ear."

Then Larry insisted on also squeezing his hand warmly.

"When I heard that man say they were chasing a boy," he remarked, "I knew what it was I'd seen scramble under the blankets; and I made up my mind that they wasn't going to get you, if we had to fight for it. Just to think of seven hulking men after one small boy. But we're too far away now for any of them to get you; and perhaps you'd like to stay aboard till we reach your home below; because we expect to pass all the way to the gulf, you see. He'd be welcome, wouldn't he, Phil?"

"Sure he would," affirmed the other, heartily, as he eyed the boy; and perhaps a dim suspicion that he might find the fugitive valuable as a guide began to flit through his mind then and there.

"We've got oceans of grub aboard; and perhaps you wouldn't mind helping out in the cooking line; because, you see, I'm the one in charge of that part of the game; while Phil, he takes care of the running gear. Anyhow, no matter, you're welcome to stay with us on the trip. We're glad to know the fellow who dared lick that big bully of a Bob Brashears, see?"

The boy let his head drop. Perhaps it was because he did not want to let these generous fellows see the tear in his eye, and of which he was possibly ashamed, though without reason.

"Say, that's right kind of you both," he exclaimed presently, when he could look them in the eyes without winking. "And I'm gwine to say yes right away. I wanted to stay up here yet a while; but I saw the town was gettin' too hot foh me; and I made a fix with a friend I got thar, so's I could know how it all came out. Yep, I'll stick with you, and be glad in the bargain."

"What might your name be?" asked Larry, frankly.

"Tony," came the immediate answer; but although it might be supposed that the swamp boy had another name besides, he somehow did not seem to think it worth while to mention the same—or else had some reason for keeping it unspoken.

"Well," remarked Phil, who had listened to the way the other spoke with more or less surprise; "I must say that if you do live in the swamp, and your folks are a wild lot, according to what these people around here say, you talk better than any of the boys we've yet run across since we struck this place. Ten to one you've been to school a time, Tony?"

The swamp boy smiled, and shook his head in the negative.

"Never seen the inside of a school in my born days till we come up here a while back, me an' little Madge. But my mother didn't always live in the swamps. Once she taught school down in Pensacola. Dad met her when he was ferryin' shingles, an' that's how it came around. She says as how her children ain't a-goin' to grow up like heathen, if they does have little but rags to wear. And so she showed me how to read, and I'm wantin' to get more books. Looky here, this is one I bought since we kim up the river," and as he spoke he drew out from the inside of his faded and torn flannel shirt a rather soiled volume.

"Robinson Crusoe!" exclaimed Phil, as he vividly remembered the time away back when he too had treasured the volume so dear to the heart of the average boy at a certain age. "Well, Tony, I'm going to make you a promise, that when I get home again there's going to come down this way a box of books that will make you happy. Just to think of it, a boy who longs to know what is going on in this big world, and kept back to spend his life in a swamp. Why, we've got a few aboard here right now, that you shall have when we say good-by to you."

Tony hardly knew whether he might be dreaming or hearing a blessed truth. The look he bent on the kind-hearted Northern lad told how his soul had been stirred by these totally unexpected acts of friendly regard.

"That's awful good of you, sah!" he murmured, as his eyes dropped again—perhaps because he felt them moist once more; and according to a swamp boy's notions it was a silly thing to give way to weakness like this.

"But whatever made you come up here, Tony, so far away from your home?" Larry asked. "You must have known how the people in this town hated your folks; and that if they found out you came from the McGee settlement of squatters they'd make it hard for you."

"Yes, I knowed all that," replied the other, slowly; "but you see, somebody jest had to come along with Madge; an' dad he dassent, 'case they had it in foh him."

"Madge—that means your little sister, doesn't it, Tony?" queried Larry.

"Yep. She's jest so high, an' she's been blind a long time. Last year a gent from the No'th that called hisself a professor, happened to git lost in the swamps, and some of our folks they fetched him in. He was took good care of, an' after a bit was guided out of the swamps. He seen Madge, an' he told dad an' mam that if only she could be treated by a friend o' his'n, who was a very great eye doctor up No'th, he believed Madge, she'd git her sight back ag'in."

Phil started, and looked more closely at the boy as he heard this; but he did not say anything, leaving it to his chum to learn all there was to know about the mission of Tony from the swamps, to the town of those who hated his clan so bitterly.

"And you brought your little blind sister all the way up here, did you?" asked Larry, with a ring of real sympathy in his cheery voice.

"Sho! that want nawthin' much," declared the other, scornfully. "I had a little dugout, which I paddled easy. I spected to stay 'roun' till the doctor he kim, which was to be at a sartin day; but yuh see they run me out. But I gotter a chanct to fix it all up. Madge, she's stoppin' at the cabin o' a man dad used to know. His name is Badger, an' he's got a boy Tom, jest my age."

"That's nice now," remarked Phil, taking a hand in the talk. "And is she going to stay there till this Northern eye doctor arrives, to perform the operation?"

"Yep; but mam guv me the money to let her into the horspittal, so she c'n stay thar, and be looked arter till she's well. Mam sets a heap of store by Madge; an' dad too, I reckon. They ain't gwine to sleep much till they knows whether the operation pans out right or not."

"But how will you know, now that you have been chased out of town?" asked Larry. "Perhaps this Tom Badger will go down the river to carry the news?"

"Shucks, no," said the other, with a flash of pride coming over his thin face; "I fixed that up all right. He's gwine to send a message to weuns just as soon as he knows what's what; and we'll git the news sure inside o' a few hours."

"But say, you don't mean to tell me there's a telegraph station in the swamps?" ejaculated the astonished Larry.

"Nope," replied Tony, instantly. "Jest a pigeon. Tom, he knows how to write, and he's gwine to tuck a little letter under the wing o' the bird I fetched up."

"A carrier pigeon, you mean!" cried Larry. "Why, how fine you planned it, Tony. Just to think of it, having the news flashed straight home, over miles and miles of swamps. But what if a hawk got your bird, what then?"

St. George Rathborne

"I tuck up three of 'em, so's to make sure," Tony made answer. "He promised to set 'em all free one after t'other, and each carryin' the news. So you see, sah, one of 'em's jest bound to sure git home."

"But see here, where under the sun did you ever get carrier pigeons? That's the last thing I'd expect to find away down in the Florida swamps," Phil asked.

"A man in Pensacola, as knowed my mam afore she married dad, sent a pair home to her last time they took shingles down thar, which was a year back. I made a coop foh the birds an' they hatched out a heap o' young uns. These hyah three is the pick o' the flock; an' I sure has hopes o' seein' one of 'em right soon after Tom he starts 'em loose."

"Well, you've interested me a heap," declared Larry. "Why, it's just like a story, you see. The good doctor comes, restores the sight to your sweet little sister's eyes; and then the glorious news is flashed home by a dove of peace and good tidings. Of course it'll be good news, Tony. Didn't the dove bring that kind back to old Noah in the ark? I'm awful glad you just happened to hit our boat when you wanted some place to hide. Why, I wouldn't have missed meeting you for a whole lot. Have you had anything to eat this morning, Tony?"

When he learned that their guest was really hungry, Larry immediately started to get something going. He drew out a little square black tin box; this, on being opened disclosed a brass contrivance which turned out to be a German Jewel kerosene gas stove. This was quickly started, and began a cheery song, as though inviting a kettle to accept of its genial warmth.

Evidently the swamp boy had never in all his life seen

anything like this, to judge from the way he gazed. Nor had he ever scented coffee that had the aroma such as was soon filling the air about them; for he could not help sniffing eagerly every little while, to the secret amusement of Larry.

All this while the boat had been speeding down the narrow but deep stream. Phil could look after the wheel and the engine at the same time; though as a rule he depended on his chum to stand in the bow, and warn him of any floating log or snag, such as might play the mischief with the cedar sheathing of the modern motor boat.

When Larry announced that lunch was ready Phil slowed down, and presently came alongside the bank, at a place where a cable could be warped around a convenient tree. For, since they were in no particular hurry, they did not feel that it was necessary to keep on the move while eating.

Larry had heated up a mess of Boston baked beans. Besides this they had some soda biscuits which had been purchased from a woman in the town; some cheese; and a can of sardines; the whole to be topped off with a dish of prunes, cooked on the preceding evening, and only partly eaten.

When Tony received his share he ate ravenously. Perhaps the boy had seldom tasted such a fine variety of food, for the canned stuffs likely to reach these squatters of the big cypress swamps were apt to be of the cheapest variety.

They were sitting thus as the lunch drew near its conclusion when, in addressing his chum in some laughing way, Larry happened to mention his name in full.

The effect upon Tony was singular. He started as though he had been shot, and immediately stared at Phil; while a troubled look came over his sallow face; just as though he had recognized a name that was being held up to derision and execration down in the settlement of the McGee squatters!

CHAPTER III

THE SQUATTERS

A short time later, and once more Larry loosened the rope that held the motor boat to the bank; so that the swift current taking hold, commenced to carry the craft down stream. Then Phil started operations; and the merry popping of the noisy exhaust told that they were being urged on at a faster gait than the movement of the stream could boast.

Tony had curled up in the sun, just like a dog might have done. He seemed to be asleep; and the two other boys talked in low tones as they continued to glide on down the winding river; now under heavy trees, and again passing through an open stretch, where the turpentine industry had killed the pines years back; so that only a new growth was coming on.

Perhaps Phil might have thought it a bit singular had he known that Tony did not sleep for a single minute as he lay there; but was from time to time observing his new friends from the shelter of his arms, on which his head lay.

Phil had reached under the deck of the boat and brought forth a splendid gun of the latest model. It was a Marlin repeater, known among hunters as a pump gun; and could be fired six times without reloading, the empty shells being thrown out

St. George Rathborne

from the side instead of in the marksman's face.

This fine weapon had been a present to the boy from his father on the preceding summer, when he had a birthday; and as yet he had found no opportunity to test its shooting qualities. Still, his father had once been something of a true sportsman, and knew more or less about the value of firearms; so that Phil never feared but that it would prove to be an excellent tool.

"I've got some buckshot shells along with me, you remember, Larry," he was saying as he guided the boat, and tried to keep her in the middle of the widening stream. "And I fetched them in the hope of meeting up with a Florida deer, or perhaps a panther; which animal is found down here. If a fellow can't carry a rifle these buckshot shells answer pretty well. I got my deer up in the Adirondacks last year with one, fired from my old double-barrel."

"How about grizzly bears and wildcats and coons?" asked Larry, not in the least ashamed to show his utter ignorance about all such matters, in his quest of knowledge.

At that Phil laughed out loud.

"The bobcat and coon part is all O. K., Larry," he said; "but you're away off when you think we're going to rub up against a grizzly bear down in Florida. They have got a specimen of the breed here, but it's only a small black fellow, and not particularly ferocious, they tell me. But we'll ask Tony about all these things later on; he ought to know."

"Yes, and perhaps he can help us go ashore, and get a fine deer once in a while!" exclaimed Larry, who loved to enjoy the good things of life almost as much as he did to exploit his ability as a cook. "Yum! yum, a real venison steak, cooked on the spot where the animal was shot—what a treat for hungry fellows, eh?"

"Wait," said the other, nodding. "You may change your mind before a great while. For instance, venison ought to hang quite a time before being eaten. I'm afraid you're going to be disappointed, Larry, and that if we're lucky enough to get a deer you'll find it as tough and dry as all get-out."

"Then things ain't all they're cracked up to be," declared the other. "I always read that things tasted just dandy in camp; and here you spoil all my illusions right off the reel."

"They taste good because the appetite is there," remarked Phil. "A fellow gets as hungry as a bear in the spring after he comes out from his hibernating. But already you ought to know that, because you're eating half again as much as you do up home. And of your own cooking too."

"That stamps it gilt-edged, A Number One," laughed Larry. "But here's Tony beginning to wake up. Come and join us, Tony. We want to ask you heaps of things about the animals of the timber and the swamps; also something about your people. You see, we ain't down here just for our health or the fun of ft. Phil here has got a mission to perform, that concerns the terrible McGee they told us about up in the river town."

Again did Tony send that questioning look at Phil Lancing; and there was something besides inquiry in his manner. Doubtless the words so carelessly uttered by good-natured Larry had stirred up mingled emotions in the breast of the swamp boy, and he was wondering what sort of a message the son of the man who now owned all that wild country below, could be carrying to the giant shingle-maker, leader of the whole McGee clan.

"If I c'n tell you anything jest ask me, sah!" he remarked, in his singularly smooth and even voice. "I sure ought tuh be ready tuh 'blige after all yuh done foh me. But I wisht you'd done never come down thisaways, case they's hard men, the McGees, an' I reckons as how they ain't got any reason tuh think kindly o' your governor."

As he said this bluntly, Tony looked squarely into the face of Phil; who however only smiled as he made reply.

"I see you have heard my name before, Tony? Well, you never heard anything bad in connection with it, I'll be bound. It's true that my father did come into possession of ten thousand acres or more of land and swamp, lying along this same little river a year or two ago. And he's taken a notion that something ought to be done to make it more profitable than it seems to be now. That's one of the reasons I'm down here. My father don't like the idea of having squatters on his lands. He wants to make a change."

Tony squirmed uneasily, and the look on his face was really painful to see. At one instant it seemed as though defiance ruled; only to give way to distress; as in imagination he saw these new-found friends, who had been so very kind to him, in the hands of his infuriated clansmen, and being roughly treated.

"Better not keep on down-river, sah!" he muttered. "They all knows that name o' Lancing. Sure I've heard many a shingle-maker curse it, an' say what he'd do tuh the new owner, if ever he dared show his face on the river. An' what they'd do tuh your dad they'd like enough do tuh you. That's why I asks yuh to turn aroun' an' go back, while yuh has the chanct."

"Why, you don't mean to say your people would try to harm

us?" asked Larry, his round face showing signs of uneasiness.

"They sure would, if they knowed his name was Lancing," replied the other, doggedly. "They's a tough lot, seein' as how they lead a hard life, an' they think they got a right to the land they built ther shanties on. More'n once the sheriff he tried tuh git his man down yonder. Sho! they jest rode him on a rail, an' warned him if ever he showed his face thar again they'd sure tar and feather him. An' let me tell yuh, he ain't come back from that day to this'n."

"Well," Phil went on, coolly, "I've heard all those things from the people of the town. They haven't one good word to say for McGee and his tribe. But somehow I've got a notion that your folks ain't as black as they're painted. And I'm banking on that idea just enough to take the risk of going on down there, even if it is bearding the lion in his den."

Tony shook his head dismally, and looked disappointed.

"Wisht yuh wouldn't," he muttered. "Yuh been good to me, an' I'd hate tuh know anything happened."

"Oh! that's all right, Tony," said Phil, cheerfully. "Nothing's going to happen—nothing bad, I mean. I'm not afraid to meet the terrible McGee face to face. I just want to tell him something that will make him change his mind pretty quick, I guess."

"And when they see that we've been good friends to you, Tony," remarked Larry, "they couldn't think to injure us. We come not in war but in peace. Phil, my chum, has got an idea he can fix up this whole matter without a fight; and that when he comes away again, there won't be a single squatter on the ten thousand acres his dad owns."

St. George Rathborne

"Perhaps yuh mean well, but they wouldn't understand," said the swamp boy, laying a hand on the sleeve of Phil. "If yuh kept your name secret nothin' might happen; but oh! just as soon as they learn that Dr. Lancing is your dad they're sure tuh go crazy. Then it'll be too late. Even the McGee himself couldn't hold 'em back then, big as he is, and the strongest man in all Florida."

His pleading did not seem to have any effect however. Evidently Phil had the utmost confidence in himself, and his mission as well. He knew what he was carrying in his pocket, and had faith to believe that it would win for him a welcome entirely the opposite of the rough greeting Tony predicted. But then Phil had never met the lawless McGees, who snapped their impudent fingers at the sheriff of the county, and did just about as they liked; owning allegiance only to their terrible leader, whose name was the most hated one known along the upper reaches of the river.

"There seems to be something of war between your people and these folks up in this section of the country," Phil remarked, wishing to change the conversation. "Has that always been so, and do they come to actual blows occasionally?"

"Huh! none o' the McGees ever comes up thisaways; they knows better. And they ain't a single critter belongin' tuh the upper river as dast show so much as the tip o' his nose down thar. They'd string him up; or give him a coat o' feathers. That's why my dad, he let me bring the little sister up; when he said as how he'd come hisself, mam and all the rest wouldn't hear o' it nohow; case they just knowed they'd never see him any more. If the sheriff didn't git him, some o' these cowards would, with a bullet."

"Your father, then, must be hated almost as much as the McGee himself?" observed Larry.

The swamp boy looked confused, and then hastily muttered:

"I reckons as how he is, more p'raps."

"And you've never been up in this region before, Tony?" asked Larry.

"Never has, sah. I wuks with the men, cuttin' shingles. It's the on'y way we has of getting money. Twict a yeah a boat creeps up the river from the gulf and we loads the stacks o' shingles on her. More'n a few times it been a tug that kim arter the cypress bunches. Onct I went down on a boat; and dad he took me tuh Pensacola. That's sure been the on'y time I ever was in a city. I got two books thar."

He said this last as though it might have been the most important part of his visit to civilization; and Phil smiled as he watched the varying emotions on the eager face of the swamp boy whom he only knew as Tony.

Then, as though he might have some reason for so doing, Phil once more returned to the subject that seemed to be of prime importance in his sight.

"Now about this big McGee," he remarked; "is he such a terrible fellow, of whom even his own family keeps in terror?"

"That's what every one says, sah," returned the boy, quickly; "but 'taint right tuh jedge a man by what his enemies tells. McGee is a big man, a giant; he's strong as an ox; and his people they looks up tuh him right smart. He's knocked a man down more'n once, with a blow from his fist; but 'twas when he needed a lesson. The McGee has a heart, sah, I give yuh my word on that. He keers a heap foh his wife and his chillen."

"Oh! then he has a wife and children?" remarked Phil, "and he thinks considerable of them, does he? Perhaps, after all, he may be more sinned against than sinning. You know of your own account that he cares for these children, do you?"

"Sure I do," replied the other, eagerly, and for the moment forgetting his caution. "I tell yuh, sah, that if it hadn't been foh all o' the lot that wrastled with him, he would a-come up hisself with the little gal, 'stead o' lettin' me do that same."

"Oh! you mean with Madge, your sister Madge?" cried Phil.

The boy nodded his head, a little sullenly, as though realizing what a mess he had made of the secret he had thought to keep a while longer, at least.

"But why should the terrible McGee bother his head about you and Madge?" Phil demanded, smiling in Tony's face.

Thereupon the swamp boy drew himself up proudly, as though he were about to announce himself the descendant of a race of kings, while he replied:

"Because, sah, the McGee is Madge's dad, an' mine! I'm Tony McGee!"

CHAPTER IV

DOWN THE SWIFT CURRENT

Evidently Phil was not so very much surprised after all, at this formidable announcement on the part of the boy with the sallow face. Perhaps he had even suspected something of the kind for quite a little time back. At least such a thing would account for the way in which he had been leading Tony along, until he unwittingly, in defending his father, gave his secret away.

From the look on his face it seemed as though the boy half feared that these new friends would turn against him when they learned how McGee was his father. He was therefore considerably surprised to have Phil reach out, and grasp his hand in a warm clutch.

"You knew my name as soon as you heard it, Tony," he said, with a smile that went straight to the heart of the ragged lad. "And ever since you've been trying to get me to give up this mission of mine. It tells me that you've already begun to think something of Phil Lancing. And it encourages me to think your father will do the same, after he gets to know me."

But Tony shook his head, as if in great doubt.

"Oh! if you knowed just how he's come to hate that name, you wouldn't dast let him see yuh," he said. "All sorts o' things has been told 'bout how your dad meant tuh chase weuns off'n his land. Some even says as how the soldiers was agwine tuh be used tuh hunt the squatters through the swamps whar they has lived always, an' which is the on'y home they got."

"All of which is a lie made out of whole cloth," declared Phil, indignantly, "my father isn't that sort of man. Why, he wanted to come down here himself and meet the McGee face to face; but he had an important lot of business on hand. Perhaps he may show up yet! And when your father once comes to know him, he'll never have cause to feel sore toward Dr. Gideon Lancing, because he happens to be a rich man."

"I've heard 'em talkin' about it heaps," said Tony, "an' they 'spect to have tuh fight sooner or later. They's a hard lot, and live a wild life. Yuh couldn't blame 'em much for hatin' the name of the man they look on as their enemy."

"Wait a little while, Tony. I'm bound to meet your father, and see if I can't change that stubborn mind of his. Perhaps I've got some magic about me. Perhaps I could show him something that would change a foe into a friend. Anyhow, all you say doesn't alter my mind a mite," and Phil smiled into the troubled face of the swamp boy as he spoke.

Larry had listened to all this with the greatest interest. While he might to some extent share the confidence of his chum, still he did not feel quite so positive about the warmth of their welcome by the lawless band of shingle-makers peopling the lower reaches of the river that emptied into the gulf.

So they occasionally chatted as they moved along down the stream. Phil asked a great variety of questions concerning the possibilities of the country they were now passing through, as a game preserve.

"They's deer tuh be had aplenty," Tony had answered, readily enough; "an' now an' then a b'ar. Cats and coons c'n be run across any old time. Once in a long spell yuh see a painter. Turkeys lie on the sunny sides o' the swales an' ridges. Then in heaps o' places yuh c'n scare up flocks o' pa'tridges as fat as butter."

"They call quail by that name down here," remarked Phil, turning to Larry; "just as they call our black bass of the big mouth species a 'trout' in Florida. You have to understand these things, or else you'll get badly mixed up. And Tony, my chum here wants to know how about squirrels; for he thinks he could bag a few of that species of small game, given a chance, with my Marlin pump-gun."

"Sho! no end o' 'em along the hamaks, both grays an' fox squirrels," replied the swamp boy; "they's a tough lot though; and weuns always boils a squirrel fust before we fries him."

"I've done that many a time myself," laughed Phil; "so I guess the frisky little nut-crackers are about the same, North and South. But they make a good stew all right, when a fellow's sharp set with hunger. I can remember eating a mess, and thinking it the finest supper ever."

A good many miles had been covered by the time the afternoon waned; although not a great deal of southing may have been made. That river was the greatest thing to curve, and twist back on its course, Phil had ever met with. He declared that in some places he could throw a stone across a neck of land into the water which the boat had passed over half an hour back.

"Makes me think of a great big snake moving along over the ground," Larry had declared as he discussed this feature of the stream with the others.

But Tony assured them that as they progressed further this peculiarity would for the most part gradually vanish, and the river, growing wider and deeper, act in a more sensible manner.

The country was certainly as wild as heart could wish.

"Just to think," Larry had remarked, "outside of a few shanties below the town we haven't set eyes on the first sign of a man all afternoon. Why, a feller might imagine himself in the heart of Africa, or some other tropical country. Look at that big blue heron wading in the water ahead, would you? There he flaps his wings, and is off, with his long legs sticking out from under him like a fishing pole."

"Which is just about what they are," returned Phil; "since he has to use them to get his regular fish dinner right along. There's a white crane; and what d'ye call that other handsome white bird that just got up, Tony?"

"Ibis. Ain't so many 'round hyah nowadays as they used tuh be. Some fellers gits on tuh their roosts and nestin' places, an' kills the birds when they got young uns. My dad just hates them critters like pizen. He caught a cracker onct as done it, an' they give him a coat, all right. He never dast shoot another bird ag'in, I'm tellin' yuh."

"Meaning that they tarred and feathered him?" said Phil, who was better able to grasp the meaning of the swamp boy than innocent Larry, to whom all such language was like Hebrew or Greek. "Well, I'm glad to hear that your father has such notions. And it tells me he isn't the savage some of these up-river people tried to make us believe. For any man who would shoot the mother birds, and leave the young to starve in the nests, just for the sake of a dollar or two, ought to get tarred and feathered! Them's my sentiments, Tony!"

"Hear! hear! ditto! Count me in!" chirped Larry, nodding his head positively; for he had a tender heart; and the plaintive cry of starving nestlings would appeal to him strongly—even though he had never as yet heard such a thing.

"I believe that a true sportsman ought to never destroy more game than he can make use of," Phil continued, for the subject was one very close to his heart. "My father taught me that long ago; and I've grown to think more of it right along. I've known men to throw trout by dozens up on the bank, when their creel was as full as it could hold. They seemed to think that unless a fish was killed there could be no fun in capturing it."

"Say, don't they call those kind of chaps game butchers?" asked Larry.

"Right you are, Larry; and I'm glad to see that you've got the breed sized up to a dot. I'd let a deer trot past me without pulling trigger if I knew we had all the meat we could use in camp."

"But just now that doesn't happen to apply," remarked the other, pointedly.

"Hold the wheel for a minute, Larry, quick!" said Phil, in a low, thrilling tone.

He instantly snatched up the repeating gun as soon as his

chum's fingers had closed upon the steering wheel. Larry turned his eyes to look ahead, for he realized that his companion must have seen something.

A crashing sound was heard. Then he had a glimpse of a dun colored object flitting through the scrub palmettoes under the pines.

"Oh! that was a deer, wasn't it?" Larry exclaimed.

Phil had lowered his gun, with an expression akin to disappointment on his face.

"Just what it was," he said; "and he got away scot free, all right, thanks to that scrub interfering with my aim. Well, better luck next time, Larry. I think I'm safe in saying you will have venison before long."

"But," interrupted the other, as he worked valiantly at the wheel, for they had come to an abrupt turn of the river, "I saw him skip past. Why didn't you shoot anyhow and take chances?"

"I might if I'd had a rifle," answered Phil; "but the distance was so far that I knew there was a mighty poor show of my bringing him down with scattering buckshot. I'd hate to just wound the poor beast, and have him suffer. If we could have come closer before he scampered off, it would have been different."

Possibly few boys would have allowed themselves to hesitate under such conditions; but as Phil said, he had been taught what he knew of woodcraft by a father who was very careful about taking the life he could never give back again.

After that Larry kept constantly on the alert watching ahead, in the hope of discovering another deer, which might be brought down by his quick acting chum.

"Of course we won't try to run along after night sets in," remarked Larry, as he noted how low in the west the glowing sun had fallen.

"Well, not if we know it," laughed Phil. "It's all a fellow can do now, with the broad daylight to help him guide this boat around the corners, and avoiding snags. Look at that half submerged log ahead there, will you? Suppose we ran full tilt on that now, what a fine hole there would be punched in the bow of the Aurora, to let the river in. No, we're going to stop pretty soon."

"That means to tie up for the night, don't it?" queried Larry, always wanting to know.

"If we can find a tree handy, which will always be the case along the river, I take it," Phil replied. "We carry an anchor of course; but I don't expect to use that till we get to the big gulf. Tony, suppose you keep an eye out for the right tying-up place, will you?"

The two chums had talked the matter over when they had a chance, while Tony happened to be at the other end of the boat; and thus decided to coax the swamp boy to don some extra clothes they had along with them. He was not so much smaller than Phil, and if he was to make one of their party they felt that it would look better for him to discard the rags he was then wearing.

Tony took it in the right spirit, and after a bath in the river that evening he said he would be only too glad to deck himself out in the trousers, flannel shirt and moccasins which Phil offered. The big red M on the breast of Larry's shirt, which was to become his property, seemed to take the eye of the swamp lad more than anything else. Of course it stood for Madison, the name of the baseball club the Northern boy belonged to; but it was easy to feel that it also represented the magic name of McGee.

Tony presently called out that their stopping place was just ahead. So Phil shut off power, after he had gently swung the boat in near the left bank. The setting pole, which every boat cruising in Florida waters invariably carries, was brought into use, and in this way the nose of the Aurora touched the shore.

Larry immediately tumbled over the side, rope in hand, whipping the same around a sentinel tree that stood close to the water's edge, as if for the special use of voyagers.

Once the boat was "snubbed" the current swung her around until her bow pointed up stream; and in this position she would rest easy during the night. But Phil made doubly sure against accidents by going ashore, and seeing that Larry had fashioned the proper sort of hitch knot with the stout cable.

"There's still half an hour of daylight, fellows," sang out Phil, as he picked up his gun, together with the belt of shells; "and while you amuse yourselves here, I think I'll take a little walk around. Possibly another deer might heave in sight, or even a wild turkey."

"Yum! yum! you make my mouth water, Phil," mumbled Larry, who was already getting out some fishing tackle, with the idea of trying for a bass in the brownish waters below the tied-up launch.

"Keep an eye out for rattlers!" warned Tony.

"You just believe I will," called Phil, over his shoulder. "I've got my leather leggins on though, which would be some protection. But I don't care to interview the fangs of a big diamondback. So-long, boys; see you later!"

CHAPTER V

WHAT HAPPENED ON THE FIRST NIGHT

When Phil walked away from the spot where the power boat was secured, with his two companions aboard, he did not mean to go far. Night would soon swoop down on the wilderness; and from former unpleasant experiences the young hunter knew what it was to be lost.

This was his first experience in Florida sport, and he knew that he had lots to learn; but he was a boy who always kept his eyes and ears open; and besides, had a general knowledge of the many things peculiar to the country.

He had mapped out a little turn in his mind. By moving directly east for perhaps ten minutes, then turning sharply north, and proceeding for the same length of time, after which he would swing into the southwest, Phil believed he might cover quite a stretch of territory, and stand few chances of missing the river.

He pushed on through patches of the ever-present saw palmetto, with its queer roots thrust out of the ground, and as large as a man's leg. Phil never ceased to be interested in this strange product of the southern zone, even if he did manage to stumble over the up-lifted roots more than once.

The pine woods proved rather open, since they had halted for the first night in a region where there was something of a swamp on one side of the river, and high land on the other. Tony had of course selected the latter for their stopping place.

Phil noticed that he had the breeze on the left as he advanced; and it was toward this quarter in particular that he kept his eyes turned; for if he was to get near a feeding deer it would have to be with the animal toward the wind.

When he made his first turn, and headed north, the conditions were still more favorable, since he was now walking directly into the breeze.

Once he heard the whirr of little wings. He had flushed a covey of quail; but as his mind was at the time set on nobler game, and the chance for a shot not particularly good, he did not attempt to fire; though naturally his gun flew up to his shoulder through the hunter instinct.

"Looks good to me ahead there?" he muttered, as he noticed some patches of green in open spots or little glades. "If there's a deer around, I ought to find him feeding at this hour of the afternoon."

With this idea pressing upon his mind he began to advance cautiously in the direction of the glades; keeping his body sheltered by the scrub, and his eyes on the alert for a moving red form.

Five, ten minutes he employed in making his "creep," but he found that it was time well spent; for as he finally reached the spot he had been aiming for, he discovered a deer within easy gunshot, calmly feeding.

Phil repressed any emotion that would have overcome a greenhorn at the fine prospect for a shot. He saw that the animal was a bit suspicious, since it frequently raised its head to sniff the air, and look timidly around.

That meant a quick shot, while the chance remained. Once the animal took the alarm it would bound away on wings of fear; and Phil knew that it was not so easy to hit a leaping deer, especially when trees and scrub intervened.

So he raised his Marlin at a time when the deer's head was lowered. Perhaps even this cautious movement may have stirred some leaf, for he saw that graceful head quickly raised. The deer was looking straight at him.

"Bang!"

No sooner had Phil fired than he sent the empty shell flying with one swift movement of the forearm; and by another action brought a fresh shell into place. Thus he was instantly ready to shoot again, so marvelously did the clever mechanism of the up-to-date firearm work.

No second shot, however, was needed. One look convinced the young Nimrod of that pleasant fact. The deer had fallen, and seemed to be kicking its last on the grass.

Phil hastily advanced, still holding his gun in readiness for instant action in case of necessity; for he had heard of wounded deer jumping up, and in a rage attacking the hunter.

When he reached the side of his quarry, however, the last movement had ceased; and Phil knew he had secured the game for which Larry had been pining so long.

"My! what a little chap!" he exclaimed. "Now I wonder if it

can be a youngster; and yet look at the full-fledged antlers, would you? But then it seems to me I was told the deer down South were all much smaller than up in the Adirondacks. I believe I can carry this fellow to the boat without any help."

He soon lifted the game, and swung it to his back. Then, managing to grip his gun in one hand, he took his bearings again, and started off.

Phil was too experienced a woodsman to easily get lost. And he had fixed the points of the compass so well in his mind that, just as he expected, he actually struck the river a short distance above the tied-up motor boat.

Larry was still fishing away, and so engrossed in playing a bass that had taken his bait that he did not at first notice the returning hunter. Having finally succeeded in dragging his prize aboard, with the help of Tony, he was made aware of the coming of his chum through low words spoken by the swamp boy.

One look Larry gave; then seeing what it really was Phil carried on his shoulders he let out a whoop that might have been heard a mile.

"Venison for supper, with fish! Wow! ain't we going to live high, though? Delmonico isn't in it with we, us and company tonight. See, I've caught three fine bass, Phil; and didn't they pull like sixty, though? My arms are real sore after the job of getting them in. And I didn't break your nice pole, either."

"Which was very kind of you, old fellow," said Phil. "Somebody please take my gun, so I can dump this deer on the ground. I bled him, Tony; but when we cut the venison up, we don't want to make a mess aboard. And that limb up yonder will be just the ticket to hang him from over-night, to keep our meat away from any prowling cats."

Larry drew in his line and put away his fishing rod, which of course was to him only a "pole." He immediately busied himself in getting ready to cook supper. And presently everybody seemed hard at work. Tony was cleaning the fish, Phil getting some slices from the haunch of the deer; and Larry peeling potatoes which they had secured in the river town that morning.

A couple of lanterns gave all the light needed when night gathered around them. And after all it was not so dark; for the moon happened to be more than half full, and being nearly overhead, shone down nicely.

Phil pounded the steaks he had cut off, hoping in this way to make them somewhat more tender. A fire was built ashore, since they had need to save their kerosene when it could be just as well done as not.

Over this Larry got busy. He had all the assistance he required; for as soon as the coffee got to boiling, the fish to frying, after being placed in a pan where some salt pork had been tried out; and the venison to browning, the mingled odors caused every fellow to realize that he was mighty hungry.

As long as he lived Larry would probably never forget that first supper in the wilderness. It seemed to him as though he might be living in an enchanted land; with that silvery moon shining overhead, the fire sparkling near by, and all those delightful dishes awaiting attention.

Food never tasted one half so delicious as it did right then; for already was Larry beginning to get the hunter's zest, what with the ozone in the air, and the prospect for happy days ahead.

And when they could eat no more there was still quite a quantity of the cooked food left over, which Larry stowed away in a couple of pans against breakfast.

With Tony's help Phil managed to draw the carcass of the deer up some ten feet from the ground. It looked quite weird swinging there in the moonlight; but Larry chuckled with pleasure every time his eyes roved that way.

He had declared the venison was all that he had expected it to be; and vowed it equaled any ordinary beefsteak he had ever eaten.

"Next time we try it, though," Larry said, "I'm going to fry a mess of those nice big onions we've got along. Always did have a weakness for steak with onions."

"Let's talk about something else besides eating," remarked Phil.

"Well, how d'ye like your coffee then, with this evaporated cream in it?" asked the cook, as he lifted his tin cup, and proceeded to drain it.

"It's all to the good, and touches the right spot," Phil laughed; and then added, to get his chum's mind off the subject: "How many more days journey lie ahead of us, Tony, before we strike the region where the shingle-makers live?"

The swamp boy seemed to consider.

"If we make good time tomorrow, it ought to be only one more day after that," he remarked, with convincing positiveness.

"Well, we don't expect to rush things," said Phil; "but since there's an ugly piece of business ahead, I mean to get it over with as soon as I can, with reason. One more night, and then we'll come in touch with your people, eh?"

"If yuh don't change your mind some, an' turn back," replied the other; with a vein of pleading in his smooth Southern voice that quite touched Phil.

He knew what influenced the swamp boy; who was fearful lest some harm befall the new-found friend who had become so dear to him, even though a span of a day would cover their acquaintance.

"How about our being disturbed tonight by some hungry wildcat that might scent fresh blood, and think to dine on our fine deer up yonder?" and Phil nodded his head up toward the swaying bundle—for the game had been partly skinned, and was now wrapped up in the hide.

"That might be," returned the other, carelessly. "All depends if thar be a hungry cat aroun'. Hear 'em, and get a shot."

"Oh! my! do you really think such a thing could happen?" exclaimed Larry, a bit uneasily as though he wondered whether an agile wildcat might not take a notion to jump into the launch while up in the overhanging tree.

"Don't worry about it, Chum Larry," said Phil soothingly. "This stationary top would keep him from getting aboard, you see. But in case you hear a shot during the night, just remember what we've been talking about."

"All right, I will," Larry observed; and later on when making preparations for sleeping he was unusually careful to tuck himself well in, and draw down the curtains close to him, fastening them securely with the grummets that were meant to clutch the round-headed screws along the side.

Phil himself was secretly wishing a hungry cat might come sneaking along, to climb up in the tree, and tackle their meat; for he wanted to have the satisfaction of saying he had shot a Florida bobcat; and in protecting their stores he could find plenty of excuses for making war on such a beast.

So he arranged things when laying down, in order to allow of a peep at any time he woke up. As long as the moon remained above the horizon, which would be until after midnight, he could plainly see that dark object swinging from the limb of the tree above.

None of them dreamed of the various things that were fated to come to pass ere the journey's end was reached. Could stout hearted Phil have had a fleeting vision of what lay before them, even he might have hesitated about going on. But he fully believed that he was carrying an olive branch of peace that could not fail to subdue the truculent nature of the dreaded McGee. And it was in that confident spirit he fell asleep.

Possibly a couple of hours may have passed when he awakened, feeling rather cramped from lying on one side so long. Before turning over, he remembered his intention to take occasional peeps up at the meat that had been swung aloft; and raising the flap of the loose curtain he cast his eyes in that quarter.

The moon was lower now, but still shone brightly. And he could without any particular trouble make out the dark object which he knew must be the suspended package of venison. Nothing seemed to be near it, save the usual branches of the tree; and Phil was about to give a satisfied grunt, after which he would roll over the other way, when somehow he became convinced that the bundle appeared much larger than previously.

Watching closely he made a startling discovery. There was some object flattened out on top of the deer, for he plainly saw it move, as though a head were being raised. And what was evidently the truth burst upon him. A wildcat had climbed the tree while they slept, and was now trying to get at the venison!

CHAPTER VI

"SAVING THE BACON!"

Phil reached for his gun. Luckily he had it close by, even though hardly expecting to make use of it during the night.

He fancied he heard a low snarking sound; possibly it may have been pure imagination; though so wary an animal as a wildcat might have detected a movement down below, where its human enemies held forth, and signified by this means its displeasure at being disturbed in a feast.

Now the gun was being carefully pushed forth, advantage being taken of the opening under the canvas cover, where Phil had released a couple of the grummets. He wondered just how he was to get the butt against his shoulder, under such peculiar conditions; but where there's a will there nearly always can be found a way; and in the end this difficulty was bridged over.

Then he thought of Larry. What a fright the sudden roar of the gun in the confined space under the canopy would give his chum. But Phil had warned him against being alarmed in case of a shot during the night.

Was the cat still there?

St. George Rathborne

Looking closely he could see a movement as though the animal might have finally reached the meat through the covering, and was busily engaged chewing at it.

"Think of the nerve of the thing!" Phil was saying under his breath, as he got ready to fire.

The report quickly followed. Phil, once he was ready, began to have a fear lest the animal take sudden alarm, and make a leap that would carry it beyond his range of vision. And the more he thought over the thing the greater became his desire to punish the beast for its audacity.

"Thunder!" shouted Larry, as he came floundering off his made-up bed, landing in a struggling heap in the bottom of the motor boat.

"Oh! no, not quite so bad as that," laughed Phil, himself gaining an upright position; and trying the best he could to throw out the old shell, so that he might have the pump-gun in serviceable shape again.

Tony seemed to be the least disturbed of the lot. Familiarity with alarms had considerable to do with it, no doubt. He had started to open the flap of the canvas cover nearest him, so that he could thrust his head out.

"What happened, Phil?" asked Larry, as he sat up on the floor of the boat.

"Why, I just saved our bacon; or to be plainer, our venison," laughed the other.

"Oh! was something running away with it, then?" demanded Larry, beginning to get upon his knees as the first step toward rising.

"Something was making way with it, which is about the same thing," replied Phil.

"W-was it a bobcat?" continued Larry.

"Listen!"

As Phil said this one word they could hear a fierce growling, accompanied by a strange scurrying sound. It came from the shore close to the boat.

"Will it come in here after us, Phil?" asked the more timid member of the firm, as he tried to find the hatchet which he remembered seeing somewhere close by at the time he lay down on his cot.

"How about that, Tony; do you think there's any danger of such a thing happening?" queried Phil, turning to the swamp boy.

"Getting weaker all the time," came the ready reply. "I think yuh give him all in the gun. Kick the bucket purty soon now."

Tony thrust the curtains more fully aside. Then he crept out and reached the shore; nor was Phil far behind him. The latter, however, not being quite so confident as Tony, insisted on carrying his Marlin repeater along. If the dying cat gave evidence of a desire to attack them, he wanted to be in shape to finish matters on the spot.

There was really no need. Even as he arrived on the scene the stricken animal gave one last convulsive shudder, and stiffened out.

"Good shot that!" remarked Tony, admiringly, as he bent

over to see where Phil had struck the midnight marauder.

"Wow! what a savage looking pussy!" exclaimed Larry, joining the others. "I'd everlastingly hate to run up against such a customer in the pine woods. Say, if a fellow like that pounced down on my back some time, what ought I to do?"

"Lie down, and roll," laughed Phil; who knew that down here in this warm country, where food is plenty, no wildcat would be bold enough to openly attack a human being without provocation.

Tony immediately started to shin up the tree, desirous of ascertaining the extent of damage done. When he came down he announced that the beast had just succeeded in tearing a way in to the venison; but had eaten very little of it, thanks to Phil chancing to awaken when he did.

So, as the night air felt rather chilly, they soon bundled back into the boat again, and sought to secure more sleep.

There was no further alarm that night, and Larry was glad when his chum aroused him by saying that morning had arrived.

The sun was beginning to gild the eastern heavens when they started to get breakfast. Larry took a look all around, after what he fancied would be the manner of an old sea dog; and then gravely announced his opinion as to the weather.

"Guess we're going to have another fine day of it. No sign of red in that sunrise; and the few fleecy white clouds don't whisper rain. You know, Phil, I'm taking considerable interest in weather predictions these days. Got an old almanac along, to compare notes. I hazard a guess first, and then look up what old Jerold says we're going to have."

"Well, how do his predictions pan out?" asked Phil.

"Oh! nine times out of ten it happens just the opposite to what he says. That's the fun of the thing. He knows how to tell what the weather ain't going to be; and to my mind that's going some. Now, what shall we eat this morning?"

"Any of those fresh eggs left we bought from that old cracker just outside the town limits?" asked the head of the expedition. "Half a dozen, you say? Good! Suppose you give us an omelet for a change. They might get broken, anyway; and we'd better have the use of 'em."

"What will you do with that awful beast out there, Phil?"

"Tony is going to look after him for me," replied the one who had shot the bobcat thief. "He says it is a very fine skin, and that sometime I'll be glad to have it made into a little door mat. He knows how to take it off, and stretch it on a contrivance he expects to make. You see, he's handy at all such things. Necessity is a great teacher. If you just had to go hungry for two whole days, Larry, I really believe you could do it."

"Perhaps I could," sighed the other; "but thank goodness, just at present there's no need of fasting, while we've got all these bully stores aboard, and that haunch of prime venison hanging up there. Suppose you drop it down, Tony, if you don't mind climbing the tree again. Two eggs apiece ain't going to fill the bill; and the taste I had of that venison last night haunts me still."

At that Phil chuckled.

"Seems to me, just before we went to bed I saw you getting away with the surplus we put in that pan," he remarked.

"Oh! that was only a little snack," replied the unabashed Larry. "This air seems to tone up a fellow's appetite some. Given a week or two of the open life, and I have hopes that my usual appetite will come back to me again."

Of course the breakfast was a success. Larry could cook, even if he did lack many of the qualities that should be found in a woodsman; and was woefully ignorant as to the thousand and one things connected with the great outdoors.

Still, Phil had hopes of him. From time to time he kept dinning certain facts into the ears of his chum. These concerned the secrets of the open, and which at times are so important to any one who dares venture into the woods.

He explained for instance, to his boat mate, just how to learn the direction of the compass from the sun, the marks on the trees, and even his watch, if put to it. He showed him how to make a fire without a match, by the use of friction, after the manner of savage tribes who never knew flint and steel, or a brimstone stick. He explained to Larry how easy it was to cook game, by making a fire in a hole until it had become very hot, and then placing the meat therein; sealing the oven until hours had elapsed; which backwoods method of cooking was really the first fireless cooker known.

In these and dozens of other ways Phil daily taught his chum. Larry evinced considerable interest in the matter so long as his comrade was speaking; but that was about as far as it went. He did not have the spirit in him; and the seed fell on barren ground. Larry would never in all his life make a genuine woodsman. But if he kept on, he might in time get a job in a restaurant over the grill, so Phil assured him, as he complimented Larry on the fine omelet.

An hour later they left the place which Larry called "Wildcat

Camp" in his log of the motor boat cruise.

Larry was full of high spirits. Indeed, it was hard for him to keep from showing his bubbling good nature at any and all times. Phil too seemed quite contented with the way things were moving along. Only the swamp boy gave evidence of increasing uneasiness.

Tony would sit there as if lost in thought, his eyes fastened on the frank face of the young fellow for whom he had come to entertain such a lively sense of friendship in the short time he had known him. Then he would sigh, and shake his head dolefully, as though he foresaw troubles arising which he would fain ward off, if only Phil would accept his earnest advice, and turn around before it was too late.

But Phil believed he had that on his person which would change the terrible McGee from a bitter enemy into a good friend; and confident in his own honorable intentions he never dreamed of turning back.

St. George Rathborne

CHAPTER VII

LARRY CATCHES THE FEVER

"Looks like there ought to be some game around here!"

Strange to say it was Larry who made this remark. They had tied up at noon, and made a fire ashore, at which the midday meal was prepared. Phil seemed in no particular hurry to proceed afterward; and Larry, who had been "mousing" around, as he called it, surprised his chum by declaring that the appearance of the country indicated the presence of game.

Perhaps the many talks of Phil were beginning to bear fruit. Then again it might be Larry rather envied his chum the glory of killing that marauding bobcat; the skin of which at some future day Phil would have made a fine mat, at which he could point, and carelessly speak of the "time when he knocked that beast out of a tree, while the moon was shining, and his companions sound asleep."

More likely than either of these, however, Phil believed his chum was yearning for a variety in the bill of fare. Quail on toast would strike Larry about right; or even rabbit or squirrel stew; provided the meat for the pot were the product of his skill as a Nimrod.

"Suppose you take the gun, and prowl around a bit!" he suggested, more as a joke than because he dreamed lazy Larry would accept the proposition.

"All right!" exclaimed the other, with surprising alacrity. "Me to do the sneaking act, and see if I can hit a flock of barns. You know I did manage to break one of those bottles you threw up that day, Phil, even if you said I shut my eyes every time I pulled the trigger. All the more credit to me. It takes a smart marksman to hit a flying object with his eyes shut. Just think what a miracle I'd be if I kept 'em open! Gimme the gun, and let me hie forth. Quail for supper wouldn't go bad; but if it should be wild turkey, why, I suppose we'll just have to stand it."

Phil hardly knew whether he was doing right to let Larry saunter forth. Even after he had handed the Marlin over, he shook his head dubiously.

"Don't go far, now," he said, warningly; "and try and be back here inside of an hour. If you ain't, we'll look you up. And remember, Larry, if you should get lost don't go to wandering everlastingly about. Just stop short, make a fire, and get all the black smoke rising you can. This fat pine makes a great smudge, you know, and might guide us to you."

"Huh! Lost, me?" cried Larry, pretending to be very indignant. "Why, after all you've been and told me it would be simply impossible! I'll know where I am every time."

"Oh! yes," laughed Phil; "just like the Indian did, we read about, eh?"

"How was that?" demanded Larry, as he buckled the belt of shells around his generous waist.

"Why, once upon a time an old Indian actually wandered around several days without being able to locate his home. That's pretty hard to believe, but the story runs that way. Then some white men came across him, hungry and tired. They asked him if he was lost, and the old fellow got mad right away. Smacking himself on his chest proudly, he said: 'Injun lost? No, Injun not lost; wigwam lost—Injun here!' And that's the way it would be with you. Now get along, and be sure you bring in the game. I changed the buckshot shells for birdshot; but put these heavy loads in your pocket in case you need them."

So Larry trotted gaily forth. He fancied he looked every inch a Nimrod in his new corduroy suit, and with the gun under his arm, carried in the same way he had seen his chum do it many a time. But then Larry did not know that the hunter who wears an old jacket, with a patch on the right shoulder where a hole has been worn by constant friction from carrying a gun, is most apt to inspire respect in the minds of those who can size the true sportsman up.

Phil was rather sleepy, for he had not secured all the rest he wanted on the preceding night. So he stretched out on the ground, and dozed.

Every little while he would arouse himself, and consult his little nickel timepiece. Tony was busy scraping the hide of the wildcat, and fixing it on a stretcher which he had ingeniously fashioned out of a heavy strip of bark, straightened out flat, and held so by a couple of sticks secured to the back.

"Time that greenhorn was back, Tony," Phil finally remarked, as he sat up. "By the way, did you hear a shot a little while ago, perhaps half an hour?"

Tony said he had, and he could also tell the exact direction from whence it had sprung.

"How far away was it, do you think?" continued Phil, seriously.

"'Bout half mile, I reckons," came the reply, without hesitation.

"The air is from that quarter too, I notice; and of course you take that into consideration when you figure on the distance?"

"Oh! yes, I know," nodded Tony.

"But half a mile—he ought to have been back before now. We'll wait a little while longer, and then if he don't show up I guess we'll just have to go after him."

Tony did not reply; but judging from the little smile that crossed his face, it was evident that the swamp boy felt pretty confident they would have to take up the hunt. He had sized Larry up pretty readily as a failure in woodcraft, and a sure enough tenderfoot of the worst type.

"No signs of him yet," announced Phil after a bit, rising to his feet; while a look of growing concern began to come upon his face. "I was silly to let him take the risk. Ought to have known Larry would bungle it, if there was half a chance. And now, Tony, what had we better do, follow his tracks, or head straight in the direction that shot came from."

"Follow trail," the other answered promptly.

"You are sure we will be able to keep on it, all right?" continued Phil.

"I think so," replied the swamp boy, with a smile of assurance; as though he looked upon such a test as of little moment; for what had he been learning all of his life if not to accomplish just such tasks?

"All right then; let's get busy."

First of all Phil dashed off a few lines on a scrap of paper, telling Larry, if he hit camp while they were absent, to settle down by the boat, and wait for them. This he stuck in the cleft of a dead palmetto leaf stem, which in turn he thrust in the ground in front of the tied-up motor boat.

Then he followed Tony into the scrub. The swamp boy walked along with his head bent slightly over. His keen eyes were doubtless picking up the plain marks made by clumsy Larry as he wandered forth in search of the coveted quail, which he hoped to adorn sundry pieces of toast that evening.

Phil too was keeping tabs on the trail, though he realized that if there arose any knotty problem that Tony could not solve, his own knowledge would hardly avail.

It was a very erratic line of tracks. Larry evidently had no particular plan of campaign marked out when he sallied forth. If he gradually bore to the left it was because of that well known failing that all greenhorns tracking through the forest, or over the open prairie, fall heir too; in which the right side of their bodies being the stronger, they gradually veer to the left, until, given time enough, they may even make a complete circle.

Tony pointed out just where the hunter, fancying he had sighted game, began to sneak up on it. Why, he could read every movement Larry had made from the marks left behind, just as readily as though he were actually watching him.

"But he didn't shoot here, after all?" said Phil.

"No, p'raps game fly away; or mebbe all a mistake," Tony replied. "See no empty shell near where he kneel in sand. He go on further, this aways," and he once more led off through the woods.

After a while Phil believed they must be close to the place where his chum had discharged his gun just once. Nor was he much surprised when Tony suddenly darted sideways, and picked up an empty shell.

"Here shoot all right; camp over thar!" said the swamp boy, pointing without hesitation through the timber; doubtless the direction of the wind aided him in thus fixing the location of the boat in his mind.

"But what could he have shot at?" exclaimed Phil. "I don't see any sign of game around here, do you?"

"Start on run fast," remarked Tony, pointing down to the ground, as though he had read that fact there in the change of the footprints.

"Then perhaps he did hit something!" exclaimed Phil. "Let's follow and see if there's any sign. It may have been only a hamak fox squirrel he saw, and thought to bag, so he wouldn't have to come in with empty hands."

"No, wild turkey!" declared Tony, holding up a feather his quick eye had detected on the ground.

"Well, however in the wide world d'ye suppose that clumsy chum of mine ever managed to get close enough to such wary game to knock a feather from it?" laughed Phil; "but he must have wounded the bird, for he's gone headlong through the woods here in full chase."

They followed on for some time. Phil began to wonder how Larry ever kept up the pace. Truly the hunter instinct must have been aroused at last in the fat boy to have caused him to thus wildly exert himself. And in the excitement he doubtless forgot all about the directions given him by his chum.

"Why, he's going further and further away from camp all the time!" announced Phil presently.

"Heap game Larry," grinned the swamp boy, who doubtless understood the new spirit that was urging the other on, with his wounded game constantly tantalizing him.

"Hark!" cried Phil, as he held up his hand warningly. "Did you hear that?"

"Help! oh! help!" came faintly from some point away ahead.

CHAPTER VIII

HELD FAST

When Larry started out upon this, his very first hunt alone, he was filled with a newborn ambition. But before he had wandered for ten minutes he began to feel the heat, and wished he had not been so silly as to imagine he were cut out for a mighty Nimrod.

Several times he stumbled over unseen roots of the ever-present saw palmetto. Fortunately he did not have the hammer of his gun raised at the time, or there might have been a premature explosion.

When twenty minutes had gone he was beginning to feel angry at himself because he had voluntarily undertaken this task, for which nature had never fitted him.

Still, he was possessed of some grit, and disliked very much the idea of showing the white feather. At any rate, he would keep away the full hour, and then try to locate the camp. Phil could not then have the laugh on him; for even the best of hunters have their hard luck days.

Several times he saw frisky squirrels looking curiously at him around some tree. He was even tempted to try and bag a few of these little fellows, for after all they were game; and perhaps more in his line than swift flying quail, or the bounding deer. But every time he thus decided, the squirrel seemed to guess his hostile intentions; for it vanished from sight, running up the other side of the live oak, and losing itself amid the abundant foliage.

Now half an hour had gone. It was really time he turned back, and headed for the motor boat. That caused Larry to wonder if he could actually figure out which the proper direction might be; so he sat him down on a log for a brief rest, while he carried on his mental calculations. When he started on again Larry actually believed he was pushing straight for camp; when truth to tell he was heading at an angle of thirty degrees away from the same.

Then, as he was stumbling along through the scrub, lo! and behold he saw a moving object ahead. What it was he did not even know as he threw the gun to his shoulder, completely shut his eyes when pulling the trigger, and blazed away.

When he looked again it was to see a big turkey gobbler fluttering along over the ground, with a broken leg and wing. Filled with great joy Larry gave a whoop, and started in pursuit. That was his undoing.

Little he thought of what a chase that stricken gobbler was giving him. In and out of the swampy places, and through the more open woods, he kept in pursuit.

There were times when he actually was so close upon the prize that he began to thrust out his eager hand, bent on capturing the wounded bird. Then, as if given a new lease of life, the turkey would again flutter away, with the panting Larry hot on the track.

More than once he was tempted to give the thing up, he felt so out of breath and exhausted from the heat and his exertions combined. And at such times the miserable bird would squat down on the ground, just as if tempting him to further labor; so once more he would start in pursuit.

The queerest part of the whole affair, as Larry himself realized later on, was that in all this time he utterly forgot that he carried a gun in which there were five more unused shells; and that a dozen times he could have made use of the weapon to finish the flutterings of the sorely stricken turkey.

Finally the desperate bird managed to flap across a swampy stretch, and drop on the opposite patch of firm ground. Larry gave the nearest approach to a cry of victory his depleted lungs would allow; for he saw that the turkey had finally given up the ghost, and died!

But how was he to reach it? As far as he could see the same stretch of quaking bog extended. In patches water even lay upon it; and the balance was black mud.

He tried it here and there, finally striking a spot where it seemed to hold up fairly well under his weight. And so, laying down the precious gun, he started out, intending to pick his way carefully over the muck, under the belief that if he looked he could see where the seeming ridge lay just under the surface.

About the time he got half way across Larry began to have serious doubts as to the wisdom of his course. He seemed to be sinking in deeper all the while, so that he even grew alarmed. Standing still for a minute to look around him, in order to ascertain whether there might not yet be found a safe causeway over to the solid ground where his wild turkey lay so temptingly, he was forced to the humiliating conclusion that it was useless in his keeping on.

Tony, having been born and brought up in the swamps, might know just how to go about the thing; but what could be expected of a new beginner? He must go back, and give up all hopes of ever laying hands on the first game that had ever fallen to his gun as a hunter. And such noble game, too!

Why, Phil would never believe his story. He would have nothing to show for it, not even so much as a feather.

To his horror, when he tried to turn around, he found that he could not lift so much as a foot; and looking down he was startled to see that he had, even while thinking the thing over, sunk in to his knees.

For the first time Larry began to tremble with fright. He had heard of quicksands, and while this black ooze could hardly be called by such a name, it was certainly a quagmire.

Perhaps it did not have any bottom—perhaps he would keep on sinking inch by inch until his head went under! And when Phil and Tony came along later, they might only learn his fate from seeing the gun on one bank, and the dead turkey on the other.

He strained with all his might. Now he managed to get one foot comparatively free; but as all his weight came on the other, that sank down two inches, instead of just one.

Wild with fear Larry started to shouting. At first his voice was strong, for he was thoroughly worked up; but after a little while he found that he was getting husky. So he stopped calling, and devoted himself to finding out whether there might not be some way by means of which he could save himself.

Possibly poor Larry exercised his mind more during the time he was held a prisoner in the clutch of that sticky mud than at any previous span of his whole existence. And he had good reason for alarm. Many an unfortunate fellow has been sucked down by the muck to be found in marsh or swamp, his fate unknown.

As Larry happened to turn his despairing eyes upward, to see whether the sun might be going down, for it seemed to be getting gloomy to him, he made a discovery that gave rise to a newborn hope.

Just over his head, and within reach of his extended hands, the limbs of a tree swung down. It was a live oak that grew on the solid ground near by; and the idea that had flashed into his mind was that perhaps he might tear enough of these same branches down to make a sort of mattress on the surface of the mud, which would even bear his weight temporarily.

Feverishly then did Larry start to breaking off such branches as came within his reach. These he carefully allowed to fall upon the mud in a heap. And he made sure to draw each down just as far as he could before breaking it loose.

But he was sinking all the while, so that he was now down almost to his waist.

Why, his hands actually touched the sticky mire when he, by accident, let them fall at his sides. If this sort of thing kept on, in less than twenty minutes it would be all over with him.

And by now he realized another discouraging fact. Even though he could succeed in making a mat sufficient to bear his weight, how was he to draw his legs, one at a time, out of that adhesive stuff?

He tried it, tried with every atom of strength left in his body; but the effort was a dismal failure. This seemed to be the finishing stroke. Larry had managed to keep his spirits up fairly well, believing that he might somehow drag himself out of his difficulty.

"I can't hardly move," he said to himself, hoarsely. "I'm stuck for fair, and all the while going down, down, slowly but surely. Oh! my goodness! what can I do?"

Looking up he saw that the largest branch was still within reach. A last wild hope flashed upon him—would it be possible for him to seize hold of this, and draw himself out of the hole?

He no sooner conceived this idea than he set about carrying it into execution. Securing a good grip, he started pulling. Strain as he would, he could not gain a particle. The only thing at all encouraging was that while he thus clung to that branch, he did not sink any lower!

Minutes passed. They seemed hours to that imperiled lad. His muscles certainly grew sore with the continuous strain of holding on so desperately, and fighting against the awful suction of the greedy mud.

How long could he hold out? Not many minutes more, he feared, for he was pretty close to the point of exhaustion now. And when nature refused to longer battle for his life he must yield to his fate.

Larry groaned at the outlook before him. Would his chums ever come? Were they still lying around the camp, filled with confidence that the hunter could redeem his boastful words, and return with the greatest of ease? Oh! what a fool he had been to start out alone. Never again would he fancy himself a woodsman, if he were lucky enough to get out of this horrible scrape.

Facing such a serious outlook it was little wonder then that Larry again burst out into shouts, that were hardly more than a mockery, it seemed to him, so hoarse had his voice become, and so incapable of serving him.

But nevertheless those shouts had served their purpose, and reached the listening ears of his comrades.

CHAPTER IX

THE SECOND NIGHT OUT

"Hold fast! we'll soon have you out of that muck!" called Phil, after he and Tony McGee arrived at the edge of the quagmire, where poor Larry was up to his waist in the oozy mud.

Their coming had given the imperiled lad new vim; it seemed to him as though his muscles were renewed, and that he could keep on gripping that branch everlastingly now, such was the fresh faith that took the place of grim despair.

Tony knew just how to go about it. Phil, seeing his lead, started to also throw all sorts of loose leaves and wood upon the surface of the mud.

So fast did they work that in a short time they had a fine covering close up to Larry himself. Thus each of them could get on one side of him, and then heave all together.

"Pull for all you're worth when we give the word," said Phil, as he took a good hold under Larry's left arm, while Tony attended to his right. "Now, all together, yo heave-o! Bully! you moved then, old fellow! Now, once again, yo heave-o! That time you came up two inches, I bet. Don't let him sink back, Tony. A third time now, all in a bunch!"

And so by degrees Larry began to ascend. The further he drew out, the easier the job seemed; until finally they dragged him ashore.

"Oh, my goodness, wasn't that a tight squeeze though!" gasped Larry, sinking on the ground in almost a state of complete collapse.

Phil saw that he was nearly all in, and so instead of scolding him on account of his carelessness, he started in to make humorous remarks, just to get his chum's mind off the terrible nature of his recent adventure.

With sticks they scraped him off, for he was a sorry sight, the black mud clinging to his fine corduroy hunting trousers as far up as his waist. But after all, that was a mighty small matter. His life had been spared, and Larry would not mind having his garments carry the signs of his narrow escape ever afterwards.

"Now to get back to the boat," said Phil, when he found that his comrade had so far recovered that he could walk; though his hands still trembled.

"But wait," said Larry, eagerly. "You surely won't think of going back without that fine turkey over there, will you? It gave me heaps of trouble, and came near costing me dear. The best revenge I can have is to make a meal or two from the plagued old gobbler that tricked me on all this way."

"Oh! Tony's got the royal bird, all right," laughed Phil. "While I finished scraping you off, so you wouldn't have such a load to carry with you, he completed the little bridge of leaves and trash, crossed on it as you should have done in the beginning, and came back. Here's your gobbler; and quite a hefty bird, too. Just lift him once, will you, Larry? And to think that he's your game! But Larry, own up now, did you see him when you fired?"

"I refuse to commit myself," replied the other, with assumed dignity that hardly went with his forlorn appearance. "It's enough that I nailed him, and he's going to fill us up for a meal or two. Lead on, Macduff! I'm able to toddle, I guess."

Tony took his bearings, and then they started. So accurately had the swamp boy judged their location, that he led them almost directly to the boat. And there was great joy in the breast of Larry Densmore when he sank down on the ground to remove his muddy trousers, so that he might not soil the interior of the motor boat.

Fortunately he had another pair along with him, so that by the time Tony had unfastened the cable ashore, and Phil turned his engine over, Larry was decently dressed again.

But it might be noticed that he was not as frisky as usual the balance of that afternoon, being content to cuddle down, and rest. Phil saw a serious look on the usually merry countenance of his chum. He knew from this that Larry had really suffered very much while facing such a doleful end. Nor did he blame him one whit.

Owing to the amount of time that had been consumed in following Larry, and getting him back to camp after his rescue, they could only expect to keep moving for a couple of hours more; when the coming of evening would necessitate their stopping for the next night.

Phil felt a strange little thrill as he reflected that possibly when yet another day had closed in they would have advanced far enough on their journey to admit of a possibility that they might run across some of the shingle-makers of the big swamps.

"Keep on the lookout for a tying-up place, Tony," he said, as he saw that the sun was sinking low.

"Not much good place along here," remarked the swamp boy, shrugging his shoulders in disgust. "Thought we get below this to-day; but stayed too long above."

"Which of course was my fault," spoke up Larry, immediately; "but even if it does look spooky around here, with all that Spanish moss hanging from the trees, we can stand it for one night."

"Sure," said Phil; "especially since we don't have to go ashore, to cook supper. We'll give our little gas stove a try-out this time, and show Tony how well it can fill the bill."

So finally Tony picked out as decent a place as he could find; Phil worked the Aurora close in; the swamp boy sprang ashore in Larry's place holding the rope; and presently the motor boat was snugly moored against the bank.

Larry thought there might be fish around, but lacked the ambition to even make a trial. All his muscles seemed sore by now; and Phil knew that it would be some days ere his chum felt as chipper as was his wont.

"Besides, what's the use?" Larry remarked, even as he mentioned the fact as to the fishy appearance of the water. "We've still got a lot of that bully venison aboard; and that fine turkey Tony is going to bake in his home-made oven ashore. Why, we'll be just filled up with grub, hang the fish! I don't care enough about them just now to bother."

Tony was already ashore, at work on his oven. Just as Phil had described to his tenderfoot chum, he first of all dug out a big hole, and started a hot fire going in it, using the dead leaf stalks of the palmetto as a beginning. Then he fed other wood, which he seemed to select carefully, until he finally had a furious red hot mass of embers there.

Meanwhile he had plucked the turkey, and made it ready for cooking.

"Time we're done eatin' oven be ready," he announced, as Larry called him aboard to supper; he having prepared the meal over the little Jewel stove, finding a way to keep things warm as fast as he cooked them.

Later on Tony drew out all the red ashes. The oven was very hot at that time. He wrapped the turkey in some green leaves, and thrust it into the hole; after which he took pains to cover the opening up, and heap earth over it all.

Of course Phil knew the principle of the thing, though up to now he had never been a witness to the actual demonstration. It acted on the same principle used with the new-fangled bottles that keep fluid hot for several days, or cold, just as it happens to be put into the receptacle. And the fireless cookers are also arranged on the same old time natural laws of retaining heat.

"Listen to the racket coming out over yonder!" remarked Larry, as they lay around at their ease later on, each having a blanket under him.

"Tony says that there's a big swamp lying over there," observed Phil. "And I warrant you he can tell what makes every sound you hear. One comes from some kind of bird squawking; another I happen to know is a night heron looking for a supper along the water's edge; then I suppose coons squabble when they meet, trailing over half sunken logs; a bobcat calls to its mate; the owls tune up; chuckwills-widows, the same birds that we call whippoorwills up North, you know, keep a whooping all the time; and there are all sorts of other noises that might stand for anything. But Tony, tell me, what is that far-away booming we hear?"

"Bull!" remarked the other, with a chuckle.

"You don't mean it?" exclaimed Larry, sitting up to listen. "Well, now, it does sound like it, too. But see here, Tony, didn't you say only a little while ago, that there wasn't a single man within twenty miles of us; unless it might be some runaway darky hiding out in the swamp to escape the chain gang?"

"That is so, Larry," replied the swamp boy, who was by now growing familiar enough with his comrades to call them by their first names. "This no reg'lar bull. It never saw farmyard. It live in water, come up on shore sometime, and holler to make 'nother bull come fight."

"Oh! you mean an alligator bull, don't you?" cried Larry, "how silly of me not to understand at first. And is that one bellowing now? He must be a giant to make such a row."

"Not so big, like ten feet p'raps," replied Tony, carelessly.

"How big do they run—about fifty feet?" asked the ignorant one; at which Tony actually laughed, the first time they had ever really heard him give way.

"Never hear of such big one, Larry. Twelve feet, some say fifteen most. And that professor he tell me 'gator that big more'n two hundred years old, much more!"

"Whew; what a whopper!" exclaimed Larry, though whether he meant the age of the saurian, or the story told to the swamp boy, he did not explain.

"One thing sure," remarked Phil, as the time drew near for them to retire, "with that blessed old swamp, and its many nasty inhabitants so close by, I'm going to keep an eye out again tonight. Perhaps we won't be disturbed by another bobcat; but I wouldn't feel quite easy unless I kept my good Marlin handy. So, boys, if you hear me making a noise again during the night, don't get alarmed. I won't be talking in my sleep, be sure of that. But listen, Tony, what animal do you suppose makes that far-away sound? If I didn't know we were cut off from civilization I'd say it was the baying of a dog at the moon."

CHAPTER X

WHEN THE SLEEPER AWOKE

"That's what it is, sah; a dawg!" said Tony, after listening for a minute.

"Then we must be closer to your people than you thought," remarked Phil.

"That cain't be so. My folks never comes up this far. Yuh see, it sorter lies atween the town up yander, an' our diggin's," the swamp boy explained.

"But how about the dog, then?" Phil went on, becoming curious. "Perhaps it might be a party from the up-river settlements, hunting down here?"

Tony nodded, and something like the ghost of a smile crept athwart his sallow face.

"Huntin'? Yes, sah, that's what it mought be," he said, quickly. "But it's game yuh wouldn't want tuh bag, Phil. Sure enough, they's coon huntin'; but not the kind that has the bushy striped tail."

Phil was quick to grasp his meaning.

St. George Rathborne

"Do you think they're after some fugitive negro? Is that what you mean, Tony?" he demanded; while Larry's innocent blue eyes began to distend, as they always did when their owner felt surprise or alarm.

"Sure," Tony asserted, confidently. "I orter know the bay o' a hound. That dawg is on the trail o' a runaway convict; an' yuh see nigh all the chain gang is black."

They all listened again. Somehow, since learning Tony's opinion, the sound, as it came welling out of the swamp far away, seemed more gruesome than ever. Phil could easily in imagination picture the scene, with a posse of determined keepers from the convict camp following the lead of dogs held in leash, and chasing after a wretched fugitive, who had somehow managed to get away from bondage in the turpentine pine woods.

"Poor critter!" muttered sympathetic Larry. "He's only a coon, and perhaps he deserves all he got; but it makes me shiver to think of his being hunted like a wild beast, all the same."

"Will they get him, do you think, Tony?" asked Phil.

"Don't know. Most always do, some time. Yuh see a feller as runs away like that ain't got no gun nor nothin'. How c'n he git anythin' tuh eat in the swamps? Now, if 'twas one o' us, as has always lived thar, we'd be able to set snares an' ketch game; but a pore ignorant coon don't know nothin'. Sometimes they jest starves tuh death, rather'n give up."

"Then they must be treated worse than dogs," declared Larry; "because no man, white or black, would prefer to lay down and die, to being caught, if he didn't expect to be terribly punished."

Tony shrugged his shoulders at that.

"Don't jest know," he said; "but I heard folks say as how 'twas a bad place, that turpentine camp, whar the convicts they works out their time. Reckon I done heard the dawgs afore, too."

"Something familiar about their baying, is there?" queried Phil.

"They sure belongs tuh the sheriff," Tony declared; "an' he must a be'n called in by them keepers tuh help hunt this runaway convict."

"The sheriff, Tony—do you mean the same fellow you were telling us about, who dared come to the shingle-makers' settlement downriver, and was tarred and feathered, or rather ridden on a rail, with a warning that he'd get the other if he ever showed his face there again?"

"Them's him," said the swamp boy, with a nod. "His name it's Barker, an' he's a moughty fierce man. But let me tell yuh, he ain't been nigh our place sence. Cause why, he knowed the McGee allers keeps his word."

"Do you suppose he'd know you, Tony?" asked Phil.

"Reckons now, as how he would, seein' as how I had tuh bring him his grub that time he was held in our place. He knowed as I was McGee's boy."

"I just asked," Phil went on, "because it struck me that if we should happen to have a call from Sheriff Barker, it might be best for you to keep out of sight. If he's the kind of man you say, he might just trump up some kind of a charge in order to carry you back with him. And once they got you in town, there's Colonel Brashears ready to make a charge against you for licking his cub of a son. How about that, Tony?"

"Reckons as how yuh has struck it 'bout right, sah," replied the other, uneasily. "This Barker, he's the sort tuh hold a grudge a long time. It sorter rankled him tuh be rid out o' the squatter settlement on a rail, an' he an' officer o' the law, with all hands a larfin' an' makin' fun of him. Never seen anybody so tearin' mad. He swore he'd come back with a company o' sojers, an' clean us out. But it's be'n a heap o' moons now, sah; an' I take notice Barker he ain't never showed up yit."

"If the runaway negro only knew that, I suppose he'd make straight for your settlement; because he'd be safe there from the sheriff?" suggested Phil.

"That don't foller, sah," the swamp boy immediately replied. "We-uns ain't gwine tuh let all sorts o' trash settle among us. The McGee ain't settin' hisself up ag'in law an' order. He don't want no fight with the hull State. More'n a few times they be a 'scaped convict hit our place; but McGee, he wouldn't allow o' his stayin' longer'n tuh git a meal, an' p'raps an ole gun, so's he could shoot game. Then he had tuh beat it foh the coast; an' was told that if he war ever caught inside ten mile o' our place he'd be give over tuh the sheriff."

"The baying seems to have stopped, now," remarked Larry.

"Reckon as how the dawgs has lost the trail," Tony explained. "Yuh see, they's so much water around hyah that heaps o' times even the sharpest nose cain't keep track o' a runaway coon. But if so be it's Barker along with them keepers, he'll keep agwine to the last minit. He's a stayer, he is, I tell yuh."

A little later they prepared to go to sleep. There was ample room for Phil and Larry to make up their primitive beds on the seats of the launch. Arrangements looking to this had been made in the beginning. True, it was always a chance as to whether one of them in turning over while he slept, might not roll off the elevated couch, and bring up at the bottom of the boat; but they provided against this by raising the outer edge of their mattress—really a doubled blanket over the seat cushions.

When Tony joined them it was a question just where he might find room to sleep. Not that the swamp boy was at all particular; for he could have snuggled down on deck, or found rest in a sitting posture; for he was used to roughing it.

On the preceding night they had tried having him occupy the bottom of the craft; and it had seemed to work well; but Tony evidently could not breathe freely when stowed away like so much cargo. So he had asked the privilege of taking his blanket, and making himself comfortable on the forward deck.

Thus it happened that his head was not far removed from that of Phil, when the latter stretched himself out on his shelf, with his feet toward the stern.

Larry was already breathing heavily, for he had the happy faculty, which Phil often envied, of going to sleep almost as soon as his head touched the pillow. Nor in making use of this word is reference made to some time in the past, when the two young cruisers were at home in their comfortable beds. Each of them owned a rubber pillow, which on being inflated, afforded an easy headrest; and during the day took up very little room, the air being allowed to escape in the morning.

On the first night out Larry had disdained to follow the

St. George Rathborne

example of his more experienced chum, who had covered his rubber pillow with a towel. Consequently Larry found that his face burned and itched all day, from the drawing effect of the bare rubber; and on this occasion Phil noted with secret satisfaction that the other was very particular to emulate his example. Experience is the best guide; and Larry would never forget the unpleasant sensation he had endured because of declining to take pattern from the actions of the "one who knew."

The last thing Phil remembered hearing ere he went to sleep was that concert from the neighboring swamp. The alligator bull had started in to bellow again, as though pleading with some rival to come around and try conclusions; and the sound was very strange, surrounded as they were by such a wilderness.

Accustomed as he was to a delightful hair mattress, of course Phil would have found it rather hard to have only a doubled blanket between the boards and himself, as Tony was doing; while he and Larry enjoyed the benefit of the cushions with which the side seats of the launch were furnished; and which, being covered with panasote, were supposed to act as life preservers should they be cast into the water. But Tony never minded it in the least. He assured them he had many times slept comfortably, perched on the limb of a tree.

Still, Phil was a light sleeper. While his chum might never awaken once during a night, Phil generally turned over every hour or so. And he had fallen into the habit, so general among old campers, of raising his head and taking an observation at such times.

Finding all well, he would lie back again, and fall into a new sleep.

He remembered doing this at least twice on this night in question. Each time it seemed to him that all was well. He could hear the various noises coming out of the swamp, and forming such a weird chorus; but they signified nothing in the way of peril. And by degrees Phil was growing accustomed to listening to the strange conglomeration.

A third time he awoke, and it struck him instantly that on this occasion he had not come out of his sleep wholly of his own accord. Something seemed to be pulling at him—it would stop for a few seconds only to go on again, and Phil noted that this tugging was wholly confined to the shoulder of his coat, which he had not discarded when he lay down, as the night air was cool.

At first a thrill passed through him. Possibly he remembered that bull 'gator with the hoarse bellow; or bethought him of certain yellow moccasin snakes Larry had noticed in the water of the stream, coming from the swamp, no doubt.

Then something touched his face, tapping him gently. Instinctively he put up his hand, and immediately felt fingers. Why, it must be Tony! Had the other thrown his arm up while sleeping, and in this way managed to arouse him; or was his action intentional?

Phil was just trying to decide which it could be, when a sound came to his ear that caused his heart to almost stop beating for a brief period; some one or some animal was certainly creeping under the curtains of the motor boat, seeking to enter!

CHAPTER XI

AN UNINVITED GUEST

Phil knew that Tony must have discovered this significant movement, and believed it his duty to arouse the one who might be depended on to meet the situation.

Could it be some wild animal that was trying to get in at their provisions? Listening, Phil believed he could catch the sound of half suppressed breathing. Then the fumbling began again, as though a body were being drawn under the canvas curtain.

It was time he were acting. So he allowed his fingers to give those of Tony a reassuring squeeze; after which he reached out his arm. His faithful Marlin must be there on the floor of the cockpit, just where he had placed it before lying down. And when he felt the familiar sensation of the cold steel barrel, he knew he had the situation well in hand.

Suddenly a wild cry arose. It had come from the lips of Tony, as Phil instantly understood; and was immediately followed by a threshing sound, as of two bodies rolling and scrambling about on the forward deck of the little cruiser.

Evidently the fearless little swamp lad had thrown himself on the intruder, whom his keen eyes had made out to be a human being, and not a panther, as Phil had at one time suspected might prove to be the case.

Phil immediately scrambled off his seat and to his feet. It was not actually dark under the cover, for the moon still shone. He could just manage to see the tumbling figures on the deck, as Tony clung to the unknown intruder with the tenacity of a cat.

Larry had rolled into the cockpit, and was trying his best to disengage himself from his blanket, which he had somehow managed to get twisted around his bulky figure. So far as any help from that quarter might go, there was no use expecting it; for Larry was certainly in a dreadful panic, not knowing what it all meant; and perhaps thinking that he was about to be kidnapped.

"Don't hit me, massa; I gives in, 'deed an' 'deed I does!" wailed a voice that could only belong to a terrified negro.

"Lie still, you!" cried Phil, thinking it best to take part in the row. "I've got you covered with a gun, and can blow the top of your head off. Not another move, now, d'ye hear!"

Of course the intruder had no means of knowing that those in the tied-up motor boat were mere boys. He heard the one word "gun," and that settled the matter.

Phil thought fast. He had no doubt but that this fellow must indeed be the man the sheriff and his posse were hunting with hounds. He was an escaped convict, from the turpentine camp, where the chain gang worked out their various sentences under the rifles of the guards.

Perhaps after temporarily eluding his pursuers the fellow had happened on the boat as it lay there alongside the bank. He

St. George Rathborne

was possibly nearly starved; and rendered desperate by his condition had determined to attempt to steal some food, taking his very life in his hands in order to do so.

Phil knew just where a lantern lay. And he always carried plenty of matches on his person, so as to be provided in case he became lost in the wilderness at any time.

So he now decided to have some light on the subject. At the crackling of his match the negro uttered a low whine, and began to struggle slightly again, possibly fearing that he was about to be shot.

"Keep still, now!" cried Tony, knocking the fellow's head smartly on the planks of the deck; for he was sprawled out on the intruder's chest.

Phil, having succeeded in lighting the lantern, held it up. The first thing he saw was the frightened face of the escaped convict. Somehow it sent a pang through the heart of the boy, for he had never in all his life looked on a human countenance that was stamped with suffering as that black one seemed to be.

"Let him up, Tony; I've got the gun, and will keep him covered!" he said.

The swamp boy obeyed. Perhaps he hardly thought it wise of Phil to act as he did, for it might be noticed that the first act of Tony was to pick up the hatchet, and keep it handy.

Larry had finally succeeded in unwinding that blanket from around his person. He was staring at them as though he could hardly believe the whole thing were not a nightmare.

"Sit up, you!" Phil repeated; and the negro obeyed.

It was plain that astonishment was beginning to share the element of fear in his face, when he saw that his captors were three half-grown boys instead of gruff men. And perhaps for the first time a glimmer of wild hope began to struggle for existence in the oppressed heart of the runaway.

"What's your name?" asked Phil, sternly.

"Pete Smith, sah," replied the other, in a quavering tone.

"You escaped from the convict camp, and it was you they were hunting with the dogs, wasn't it?" the boy went on.

"Reckons as how 'twar, sah."

"How long ago did you run away?" Phil continued, bent on finding out all the circumstances connected with the case before deciding what to do.

"I dunno, 'zactly, sah. Mout a ben six days. 'Pears tuh me like it ben de longes' time eber. Ain't hed hardly a t'ing tuh eat in all dat time, massa. Jest gnawin' in heah, an' makin' me desprit. Clar tuh goodness I knowed I must git somethin', or it was sure all ober wid me. 'Scuse me, sah, foh breakin' in disaway. I'se dat hungry I c'd eat bran! But if so be yuh on'y lets me go I'll neber kim back ag'in neber."

"But you would get something to eat if you gave yourself up to the sheriff?"

The negro shuddered.

"I sooner die in de swamp dan do dat, honey," he said, between his white teeth. "Dey got a grudge ag'in me ober dar in de turpentine camp, 'case I took de part ob a pore sick niggah what was bein' whipped, 'case he couldn't wuk. Dey

St. George Rathborne

says it's laziness, but I knowed better. He died arter dat. But de head keeper, he got it in foh me, an' he make it hard. I runned away at de fust chanct; an' I jest shorely knows dat he next door tuh kill me if he gits me back."

"What were you there for?" asked Phil, feeling more kindly toward the wretched fugitive after hearing what he said, even though it may not have been wholly true.

"'Case I war a fool, massa; I 'mits dat," returned the other, humbly. "Cudn't nohow leab de juice alone. I libed in Tallahassee, an' uster be a 'spectable pusson till I gits drinkin'. Den I got inter a row, when a man was hurted bad. Dey sent me to de camp foh a yeah; an' it ain't half up yit. But I'se gwine tuh gib dem de slip, er drap down in de swamp, dat's what."

"Larry," called out Phil, "wasn't there a lot of stuff left over from supper?"

"Right you are, Phil. Shall I get it out?" asked the other, whose heart had been touched by what he heard; for Larry was a sympathetic sort of a chap, who could not bear to witness suffering, and might be easily deceived by any schemer.

"Yes," Phil went on, quietly. "This poor fellow is pretty hungry. We'll feed him first; and while he eats decide what we had ought to do about his case."

"Oh! bress yuh foh dat, young massa!" exclaimed the man who had been chased by the dogs and the sheriff's posse. "I done nebber forgits yuh, nebber. An' if so be I is lucky enuff tuh git out ob dis scrape I 'clar tuh goodness I nebber agin touch a single drap o' de bug juice. It done gets me in dis trouble foh keeps, an' it ain't nebber ag'in gwine tuh knock me down!"

"That sounds all right, Pete," remarked Phil, "if only you can keep your word. If you got clear you could never go back to Tallahassee again?"

"No sah, not 'less I sarve my time out. It's disaway, sah. I done got a brudder ober near Mobile, an' I war athinkin' dat if on'y I cud get away I'd go tuh him. Den in time he'd send foh my wife and de chillen tuh come ober."

"Oh! then you have a family, have you? How many children, Pete?" asked Phil.

"Seben, sah, countin' de twins as is on'y piccaninnies yet."

"Good gracious!" exclaimed Larry, who had been eagerly listening while getting the leftover food out of the place where he had placed it. "What a crowd! And how could they get a living all the six months you've been in the turpentine camp, Pete?"

"Dunno, sah," replied the negro; "specks as how Nancy she dun hab tak in de washin' ag'in. Ain't dun nothin' ob de sort dis ten yeahs; but she kin do hit right smart, sah."

That was the last word Pete could be expected to speak for some time; for he was busily engaged stuffing himself with the food Larry thrust before him.

It was a singular sight, and one that Phil would doubtless often recall with a lively sense of humor. The lantern lighted up the tent of the motor boat, showing the emaciated black devouring the food about like a starving wolf might be expected to act; and the three watching boys, Phil still gripping his Marlin, Tony the hatchet, and Larry another tin dish with more "grub."

Meanwhile Phil was wondering what they ought to do. He did not like to break the law; but it seemed to him that in this case he would be amply justified in assisting the runaway convict. He had surely worked long enough to have served as atonement for his crime; and the call of those seven little children was very loud in Phil's ears.

So he made up his mind that he would place a small amount in Pete's hand before sending him away, besides some more food. And he might at the same time be given a hint that if he only headed directly south along the river, the sheriff would not be apt to follow him far, since he dared not tempt the terrible McGee by infringing on the territory of the squatter chieftain.

So they waited for the hungry man to eat his fill. And Pete, now that he no longer felt the pangs of approaching starvation, looked at Phil out of the corners of his eyes, as though trying to guess what the "young massa" was planning to do about disposing of his case.

CHAPTER XII

THE SHERIFF AND HIS "DAWGS"

"Do you see that package, Pete?" asked Phil, after he had talked with Larry for a few minutes, and pointing at a bundle the latter had made up.

"Yas, sah, I does."

"Well, I'm not going to tell you to take it; but after you're gone, I expect to find it missing. Do you think you understand?" asked the boy, grinning.

Pete looked puzzled, and scratched his woolly head.

"Yuh 'pears tuh not want me tuh take hit; and den ag'in yuh 'spects me to kerry hit off when I'se gwine away! Yas, sah, I sees what yuh means," he answered; though the blank look on his dusky face belied his assurance.

"You see," Phil continued, soberly; "if the sheriff should happen to come along we would tell him somebody had taken a package of food from the boat during the night. Understand? His dogs would be apt to pick up your trail here, anyhow; and that might be a give-away."

St. George Rathborne

"Oh! yas, sah, I gits on now," said the late prisoner eagerly. "An' it sure is a good thing foh me as how I runs acrost yuh gemmons dis same night. On'y foh dat I done drap in de swamps. I takes de grub, but I don't let you-uns knows hit."

"And when you start off, circle around and make for the south," Phil went on. "Perhaps, now, you may have heard of the McGees, who make shingles down below? Well, this boy is Tony McGee. If you're lucky enough to get to their settlement, which is on the river, he'll help you further. Here's a little money for you, Pete. I'm giving it to you just because you say you're going to turn over a new leaf if you get safe to Mobile. And perhaps some time I'll look you up, or write to your brother; because we're interested in that family of yours. What's his name, Pete?"

"Oscar Smith, in keer ob Mistah Underhill, sah. An' I suah is mighty much 'bliged tuh yuh foh dis. I's gwine tuh do what yuh tells me; dough I war a tryin' tuh git away by keepin' tuh de west."

"Well, you'll have a better chance by going down river, and I'll tell you why, Pete;" after which Phil explained how the sheriff of this county in Northern Florida had reason to shun the neighborhood where the fierce McGees held forth.

"If I knowed dat afore, massa," said the negro, earnestly, "I done be down dar by now, an' alarfin' fit to die at dat sheriff. But I make a circle 'round right now, an' git a start. I done feels dat much better sense I gets a squar' meal dat I kin keep a movin' 'long all right smart de rest ob de night."

"Then perhaps you had better be getting along now, Pete," said Phil. "You see, we can't tell but what the posse might happen on us any time; and the further you're away when that comes to pass, the better. Shake hands with me, Pete.

And don't forget that we believe you when you say you're meaning to walk a straight line after this."

The astonished fugitive had tears running down his thin cheeks when he felt the warm hearty clasp of Phil Lancing's hand. Nor was Larry going to be left out.

"Shake with me too, Pete," he said, thrusting his chubby hand out. "I haven't said much, but to everything my chum remarked I'm on. And I cooked that grub, Pete. Good luck to you! I hope you've had your lesson, and it's never again for yours."

"Now we'll turn our backs, while you disappear, Pete; so none of us can see you go," said Phil, suiting the action to his words.

"God bress youse, honey, bofe ob youse!" the man muttered, brokenly.

They heard a movement, a shuffling sound; then presently all became silent once more, and laughingly the boys turned around.

"It's gone!" declared Larry, pretending to be greatly surprised. "Some miserable thief has come, and swiped a lot of our grub! Just think of the colossal nerve of the thing, would you, Phil?"

"Let's go to sleep again," was the only remark of the other, as he started to fasten down the bottom of the curtains.

"But suppose the sheriff drops in on us?" remarked Larry, who looked forward to such a possibility with a little of dread.

"Let him come," chuckled Phil. "You can tell him how we had a package of food taken. He'll understand then what his dogs have found, when they strike the scent of Pete. But I expect that the fellow will find plenty of ways for killing his trail between now and morning. He's got a new lease of life, Pete has; and mark my words, no sheriff's posse is ever going to overhaul him from this on."

So saying Phil began to make himself comfortable again. Larry proceeded to fix his own bed afresh; and when he pronounced himself ready his chum put out the lantern.

In all, not more than half an hour had elapsed since Phil felt that first touch from the swamp boy; and yet how much had happened in that short time. The Northern voyagers had passed through a new and novel experience; and there was Black Pete hastening through the woods, and through the swamps bound south, with hope once more filling his troubled breast.

There was no further alarm during the remainder of that night, and the boys were getting breakfast when Tony uttered an exclamation.

"Look! they are comin' down below! That is Barker at the head!" he muttered.

"Drop down in the bottom of the boat, Tony," Phil hastened to say; for it had all been arranged beforehand what their programme might be.

Larry jumped ashore to unfasten the cable, while his chum hastened to pay attention to his motor, so as to get the power on without delay.

Some distance away they could see a party of men

advancing. In front trailed a pair of tawny hounds, straining at their leashes, and evidently following some sort of trail.

A distant shout announced that these parties had discovered the boat; but the boys at first paid no attention to the hail. It was only after they had started from their late landing place that they pretended to have discovered the coming file of men; and Phil answered their shouts with a wave of his hat.

The sheriff was a typical Southerner. He wore a broad-brimmed hat; and had on a long coat; which, being open in front disclosed the heavy revolver which he carried next his hip.

Each one of his three companions had a gun of some sort. Possibly they were the guards from the turpentine camp, searching for the fugitive convict. Taken all in all the quartette of men presented a very fierce appearance; and Phil felt relieved to know that poor Pete was not fated to fall into their clutches. The fugitive had given them a heap of trouble, and in case of capture could expect little mercy.

The sheriff stepped to the edge of the bank, and made motions as though he wished the voyagers to come in; but Phil had no intention of doing so. He really feared that the law officer might be tempted to carry Tony off, just to get even with his father, the terrible McGee, whom he did not dare face again.

Phil did reverse the engine, however, so that the Aurora might drift slowly past the spot where the sheriff was standing. Plainly the other desired to have a few words with those aboard.

"Hello! gents!" called the officer, with his hands forming a megaphone, so that his voice might carry the more readily.

　　　　　St. George Rathborne

"I'm the sheriff of this heah county; and this is my posse. We's huntin' a desprit convict that got loose from the camp a week back, by name Pete Smith. He's been headin' up thisaway, as the dogs allow; and p'raps now yuh might a-seen somethin' of him."

Phil pretended to look at Larry as though surprised.

"I bet you it must have been him, Larry!" he said, in a voice loud enough to be heard on shore; and then turning to the sheriff he went on: "Some sort of critter sneaked into our boat last night, sir, and made way with a lot of our grub. Guess it must have been the runaway you mention."

"And my goodness! did you hear him say it was a desperate convict, Phil?" cried the innocent Larry, showing all the signs of alarm. "Why, he might have murdered us while we slept! Oh! what a narrow escape!"

They were now opposite the sheriff, and still drifting with the current, though held back by the turning of the screw.

"Say, what's that about a thief gettin' away with some of your grub?" called out the officer, excitedly. "Whar was you campin' at the time? Didn't we see you tied up tuh the bank yonder, whar that palmetto bends down like? Tell me that, younkers! It's a heap important, yuh see, that my dawgs pick up the scent fresh, though I spect they's on to it right now."

"Yes, we spent last night there, Mr. Sheriff, right where you see that palmetto. Hope you have all the luck you deserve!" Phil sent back over the widening water.

"You'd better look sharp below aways. They's a hard crowd down in that region, the McGee clan o' law breakers and squatters. They'll clean yuh out, if yuh stop off nigh 'em.

That's a warnin', younkers. If so be yuh meet old McGee, tell him Bud Barker ain't forgot, an' in time he's acomin' back!"

Tony could hardly keep from rising up, and shaking his fist after the enemy of his father, when these threatening words floated to his ears. But Phil pulled him down before his presence was discovered by the sheriff.

The last they saw of Barker he was pushing after his dogs, pellmell, doubtless in the belief that he would get on the track of Pete again when they arrived at the palmetto tree.

"Do you really suppose that what he says is true, and Pete's a regular pirate?" asked Larry, in a troubled voice.

"Well, not any so you could notice," laughed Phil. "In fact, after seeing the make-up of the fierce fire-eating sheriff, I'm more than ever glad I gave poor old Pete the glad hand, and helped him on his way. Perhaps he may not have such a raft of piccaninnies as he said, but anyhow I'm pretty sure he deserved to be given one more chance to make good."

"Oh! I'm so glad to hear you say that, Phil," cried Larry. "I was afraid that we had made a bad break. But, my! wasn't Mr. Barker a fierce looking gent, though?"

CHAPTER XIII

IN THE CYPRESS COUNTRY

During the morning they talked often of the occurrence of the previous night. Phil no longer felt any qualms of conscience, on account of what he had done. And he really hoped Pete would get clear of the posse. There had been something in the face of the negro that impressed both boys with a sense of his honesty. He had been sent to the convict camp simply because he was unlucky enough to be in a fight. Had he been a common thief it might have looked different to Phil.

And while Tony McGee might not be able to grasp all the fine points in the matter, he could understand that these two new friends of his had warm, boyish hearts; and he often looked at them with growing affection when neither Phil nor Larry believed he was at all concerned about their affairs.

Then that old troubled expression would flit back again, to hold dominion over Tony's face. That was when he tried to imagine what his father's actions might be, after he learned that one of these lads was really the son of Dr. Lancing, the rich land owner, against whom he had so strong a grudge that he would have been sorely tempted to kill him, did the millionaire but venture into the land of the squatter shingle-makers.

They tied up again at noon, taking Tony's advice. Phil could plainly see that the swamp boy, acting as pilot of the little expedition, was trying to time their progress so as to hit a certain place toward nightfall.

"What d'ye think of it?" asked Larry, when Tony having wandered off with the gun to see if he could find some "partridges," the two could exchange words without being overheard.

"About Tony, do you mean?" queried his companion, easily guessing what was worrying Larry.

"Yes. He asked us not to leave here until about the middle of the afternoon; and then he sprung that idea on us, of stepping out to see if he could scare up any game. You don't imagine for a minute, do you, Phil, that he means to betray us to his friends, and get us into trouble?"

"Rats! You don't dream of believing that yourself, now. But I saw just as you did, that he wanted to hold us here a certain time. And it wouldn't surprise me one little bit if Tony failed to come back until a couple of hours had gone," and while saying this Phil looked wise, which fact struck his chum as particularly exasperating, seeing that he was so consumed with curiosity.

"Then do take pity on me, and tell me right away what you think," said Larry; "because I can see in your face that you've guessed something."

"Well, of course you've heard Tony try to convince me lots of times that it would be foolish in our stopping off to see his father?" Phil said to begin with.

St. George Rathborne

"Yes, I have," replied Larry, promptly. "First of all he wanted us to turn back. Then, when he saw that you just wouldn't, he asked why not keep right on past his place."

"Just so," remarked Phil. "And I've got a notion right now that Tony is holding us back so that we will just have to do some traveling after dark tonight. Perhaps he'll find some excuse for it, by saying there is no decent stopping place. And in that way the boy may hope to coax us past the dangerous point where the squatters have their settlement."

"But you won't consent, Phil; I just know you too well to believe it," cried Larry.

"Well, not so you can see it," came the positive reply. "When I embarked on this cruise I knew just what I was up against. I understood that McGee was feeling bitter against my dad; but I believe the message I'm carrying him will knock all his animosity to flinders. And not even Tony must upset my plans."

The time crept on. An hour had passed since Tony went away. They had heard several distant shots in quick succession, and Larry was filled with hope that his craving for "quail on toast" might be finally made an accomplished fact; though just where the latter article was to come from might have puzzled any one, since their last scrap of bread had long since vanished from mortal view.

Another hour seemed almost exhausted, and Larry began to grow uneasy.

"He's got your new gun along, Phil," he remarked.

"That's so," smiled the other, who did not seem one whit disturbed by the non-appearance of the swamp boy; "but don't you believe that cuts any figure in his keeping away. I've been studying Tony right along, ever since we met him first; and I'd stake a heap on his fidelity. He has come to care for us, too. I could see that by the way he watches us, and the light in his eyes at times. But there he comes right now, Larry; and he's holding up some game you like right well."

"It's quail all right, and a fine bunch of the little darlings, too!" exclaimed the cook of the expedition, his face relaxing into a happy grin; and all doubts immediately vanished from his mind.

Tony came slowly into camp. Phil noticed that there was a serious look on his face, as though more than ever the swamp boy might be troubled in his mind. Which fact gave Phil a rather startling idea.

Could it be possible that Tony had met with any of the squatters during his little side hunt? And suppose this to have been the case, what had happened between them? Of course they must know that Tony had gone up-river with his little blind sister, so that his presence near the home settlement would arouse both their curiosity and suspicions.

They must also notice the wonderful pump-gun he was carrying; and that again would be likely to cause them to demand an explanation. Would Tony tell all that had happened to him? And might the news be thus carried ahead of their coming to the terrible McGee, that the son of the rich man he hated so bitterly was even now in his power?

But Tony said nothing. He was far from being talkative at any time, and just now he seemed to shut up as "tight as a clam," as Larry expressed it aside to his chum.

They started down the now wide stream. Since the boys first

commencing this eventful voyage two days back, the river had received many additions in the way of smaller creeks, so that it was now pouring quite a volume of water along toward the gulf.

And it was easy to see from the nature of the frequent swamps bordering the banks that they were drawing near the great cypress belt where the shingle-makers held forth in all their glory, defying eviction on the part of any owner of the territory.

It was about the latter part of the afternoon when Larry called attention to a man on the shore. He was standing on a hamak, and held an old gun in his hands, as though he might have been hunting up this way, and his dugout not far off.

The fellow was far from prepossessing looking, to say the least. His garments were of dingy homespun, and his beard gave him the appearance of a tramp. But of course Phil realized that he must belong to the settlement toward which they were gradually drawing closer with every mile passed over. And if so surely Tony would know him.

He noticed that the man was staring at them as they glided past, with the motor slowed down to its lowest ebb; as Tony had requested that they only keep with the current. And turning toward the swamp boy he saw him make some sort of sign to the man—it might be merely a wave of recognition; and again there may have been a deeper significance connected with it.

"You knew him, then, Tony?" asked Phil, trying to seem indifferent.

"Oh! yes, sure," replied the other, quickly. "That was Gabe Barker."

"Barker!" exclaimed Phil, "any relation to our friend the sheriff, now?"

"Yep, that's the funny part o' it," replied Tony, with a slight smile. "Gabe an' the sheriff be full cousins. But all the same, Gabe he helped to carry the pole when they ride t'other Barker out o' the settlement. They has a feud you see, his fambly an' that o' the sheriff."

"But Gabe is one of the McGee clan now, isn't he?" pursued Phil.

"He's be'n, nigh on seven year," Tony admitted. "Think he licked the father o' the sheriff, and hed tuh cut stick an' run afore they got 'im."

"Why d'ye suppose he didn't call out to you?" asked Phil; who really considered this the most sinister part of the entire proceeding; for according to his way of thinking it would have been the natural thing for a man to have done under such circumstances.

Tony allowed that queer little smirk to creep over his face again.

"Gabe he would like to much, on'y he couldn't," he said.

"Why, I didn't see anybody stopping him!" ejaculated Larry.

Tony made a movement toward his mouth, and then observed:

"Gabe he not say much now for five years. Used tuh curse more'n three men. Then a tree he was cutting down fell wrong way. Gabe he caught underneath. Bite tongue off and near die when McGee find him. So he makes talk with hands since that time."

"Oh! what d'ye think of that, now?" cried the wondering Larry. "Pretty tough on that long-legged Gabe, for a fact. No wonder then, he didn't call out to you, and ask all those questions I could see on his face."

"Tony, do you suppose now that Gabe came up the swift river in his dugout, which I noticed floating on the water near where he stood on that rise?" asked Phil, with a reason for the query.

The swamp boy looked uneasily at him, but answered at once.

"No, current too strong. We come this far through swamp. I paddle so when I take little sister up-river. That place whar Gabe stand hide entrance to swamp."

"And how long do you suppose it would take Gabe, if he started right away, to get back to the settlement?" Phil continued.

"After sundown, an' afore dark," the other answered. "River turn many times, but through swamp it is easy to go straight away."

"Then unless we started up, and ran for it, Gabe could get there sooner than our motor boat; is that a fact, Tony?"

"Yes," replied the swamp boy, with a sigh, "Gabe get there first, anyhow!"

CHAPTER XIV

LARRY PICKS UP SOME MORE POINTERS

Although the boys had left their stopping place that morning in something of a hurry upon sighting the advancing posse of the sheriff, it must not be supposed for one minute that they had forgotten all about the treat they had been anticipating in the way of breakfast.

Larry had it firmly fixed in his mind; and as soon as he could coax Tony to go ashore, the swamp boy and himself had opened the primitive oven in which they had placed the noble turkey.

It was found done to a turn, cooked beautifully by the heat that had been retained all through the night. Possibly the boys missed the customary brown, outside appearance, such as they had always seen in a fowl roasted in an ordinary oven; but for all that it was delicious.

Larry had gone into ecstasies when enjoying the meal; which was eaten while on the way down the river; the coming of Barker and his following having started the expedition suddenly.

And many times during that day had Larry referred to the

great luck that had befallen him during his grand hunt. He would never cease to plume himself on having actually bagged that king bird of the American forest, and which is usually so timid that only the most experienced hunter can secure such a trophy.

"And," he would say, as he picked a drumstick at noon with the keenest of relish, "our good luck didn't stop with my having bagged the gobbler, either."

"That's a fact," Phil had remarked; "our coming on the spot had considerable to do with this lunch we're making right now. Because, only for that, it might be a funeral feast instead of a joy spread, eh, Larry?"

"Well, that's just about right, Phil," the fat youth had replied, turning just a shade paler than usual, although on account of his rosy hue this fact could hardly be noticed, to tell the truth; "but I wasn't thinking of that; and please don't mention it too often, for it's apt to take my appetite away."

"Then tell us what you did mean?" demanded his chum.

"I was thinking first of all how fortunate for us that the delicious odor of our cooking turk didn't ooze out from the oven," Larry went on.

"Oh! now I catch on to what's on your mind," laughed Phil. "You're thinking of our colored friend, Pete Smith, the chap with the seven piccaninnies?"

"That's what I am, Phil. What if he had caught the odor of that noble bird in his half starved condition?"

"Whose—the bird's?" queried Phil, wickedly.

"Oh! no, you know I mean Pete," replied Larry, quite unruffled. "Don't you suppose he'd have followed his nose, and discovered how we'd placed the turkey away so neatly? And he'd have uncovered him, and run away with the whole show. That would have not only cheated us out of our breakfast and lunch; but have also lost us a chance for doing a noble deed."

"Hear! hear! I see you're bringing your Boy Scout training down to Florida with you, Larry. And I wager you never let a sun go down without having done something to make a fellow critter happier. But stop and think, it was only midnight when Pete gave us that call, wasn't it?"

"Somewhere about that time, I guess; but why?" Larry asked.

"Don't you see," Phil went on positively; "the oven couldn't have more than half done its work by then; so even if Pete had gobbled the gobbler he'd have had to eat him partly cooked. Not that Pete would have objected very much to that, for he was too near the starving point to kick. Now, my opinion is, we had greater luck because we dug up our breakfast as early as we did."

"How's that, Phil? What has the early bird got to do with the worm; or the worm with the early bird, as it is in this case?"

"Why, you must remember that we had to quit in something of a hurry," laughed Phil. "If our turkey was still in the oven don't you suppose those dogs would have nosed it out in a jiffy after they arrived? And we couldn't turn back to claim our game. That posse would have feasted on the fruits of your great hunt."

In spite of Larry's love for argument, based upon the fact that he expected to some day become a lawyer like his father, he was compelled to admit that in this case Phil had the best of it.

And so the bones of the turkey were polished off in the middle of the day; with every one declaring that it had been a great treat. Larry kept the two drumsticks as well as the wings of the gobbler. Possibly he might many a time feel a queer little sensation creeping up and down his spinal column as memory carried him back again to that slough, where the treacherous black mud was slowly but surely sucking him down.

And now the sun was creeping closer and closer to the western horizon; and they must soon come to a stop for the night; unless, as Phil rather suspected, Tony had conceived some sort of wild idea as to influencing them to keep right on, so that he could run them past the settlement of the shingle-makers in the darkness.

Of course there was bound to be a moon, for it even now hung low in the eastern heavens, being well on toward the full; and, as boys accustomed to the woods well know, a full moon always rises above a level horizon just at sunset. But clouds floated in patches across the sky, and it might be they would obscure this heavenly luminary long enough for Tony's purposes.

But Phil was equally determined not to let the swamp boy try to run them past. He had come far to carry out his purpose; and could not bring himself to believe that it might fail utterly. Much as he had heard about the fierce nature of the giant, McGee, chief of the clan, he had faith to believe that even such a rugged and almost savage character might be subdued, if one went about it in the right way.

"We must be looking for a place to haul up, Tony," Phil

finally said, in his most determined tone.

The swamp boy looked almost heart-broken upon hearing him say this. He gritted his teeth together, and frowned. Phil knew what must be passing in his mind; and how poor Tony felt, that in obeying the wishes of this new friend, he was acting as a decoy, to betray the son of the hated Dr. Lancing into the hands of those who would treat him roughly.

Tony shook his head and sighed. Then, as if making up his mind that there was no other course for him to pursue, he tried to smile cheerfully. Perhaps he still hoped that if the worst came, he might find another arrow in his quiver to use. Perhaps he relied somewhat on the influence of his mother, she who had once been a school teacher in a city, before she came to marry this chieftain of the McGee clan.

"Just as yuh say, Phil," he remarked, meekly. "If we have tuh tie up, reckons as how it could be did 'round hyah as well as anywhar else. Yuh see thar's swamp nigh everywhar 'bout, now—nothin' but cypress in this part o' the kentry. So, when yuh say so, we'll get a hitch 'round a tree, an' stop."

"Looks to be a likely place ahead there," remarked Larry, who had been amusing himself with a pair of marine glasses Phil had brought along with him; and which promised to be particularly useful, once the motor boat reached the big waters of the gulf.

"Yep!" sang out Tony, who had such keen vision that he found no need of glasses to assist him, "they's some land thar too, which makes it right decent. If so be yuh feel that yuh must stop, Phil, that's a shore good place."

And so they headed in for the landing selected, after navigating the stream for a short time longer. The sun had not yet

St. George Rathborne

gone down, though under the tall cypress trees, with their great clumps of gray hanging Spanish moss that looked like trailing banners, it was even then beginning to grow a little dusky.

Gently running alongside the bank, the Aurora came to a stop. Larry with his rope was quickly ashore, and securing the cable to a convenient tree. Then they let the motor boat swing around, so that her prow headed up-stream; after which she was apt to lie easy all night, with the current gurgling past, and singing the everlasting song of the running water.

Larry was for going ashore and making a fire, but Tony begged him not to.

"They find us soon enough, without hurryin' it 'long that way," he said.

"Oh! well," Larry replied, "I suppose we can use the bully little kerosene gas cooker tonight. It's a howling success, according to my mind; and I'm only wondering why you didn't get a second edition while about it, Phil."

"Because it was new to me," replied his chum; "and while I'd heard a heap about it, I thought I'd like to try the thing out first. But I give you my word I'm going to have another as soon as I can send for it. And never again shall I go into camp without one along. Think of the rainy days when I've had to go hungry because all the wood was soaked; when with such a treasure in the tent you could cook to your heart's content."

"Then you give in to Tony, and say no fire ashore tonight?" asked Larry.

"Well, yes," was Phil's reply. "It's pretty warm anyhow to cook over a blaze. And perhaps after all it might be better for me to drop into the village of the McGee, of my own free will, rather than be taken there, apparently against it."

Again Tony sighed. Perhaps he felt that there was small chance of their passing that night so near the settlement of his people without having unwelcome visitors. Perhaps he knew only too well how the mute Barker must ere now have arrived among the shanties of the shingle-makers with his astonishing news; and that many dugouts would soon be scouring the river in search for the remarkable motor boat on which he, Tony, seemed an honored guest.

"I wonder if I could catch any fish here?" remarked Larry, who could not forget the success that had attended his previous efforts in the "hook and pole" line.

"Plenty everywhere along here, I should guess," remarked Phil. "So suppose you get busy, and see if you can't pull up a supper for the crowd. Fact is, old chum, you're rapidly developing into a second class scout. When you get back North you will know so much that they'll just have to get you a medal to wear. And the marks on the sleeve of your khaki jacket will about reach from your shoulder to your elbow, you'll qualify for so much."

"Aw! quit jollying me, Phil," chuckled Larry, who nevertheless seemed to enjoy the novel sensation of being complimented on his newly acquired knowledge in the line of woodcraft.

He was soon busily engaged untangling his fishing line, while Tony went ashore to hunt for grubs in old logs; and Phil employed himself otherwise. From time to time the chums exchanged a few words, with Phil taking Larry to task for persisting in calling his jointed bamboo fishing rod a "pole!"

"That goes well enough with the country boy, who has only a long bamboo pole, with the string tied at the end," he said, with the air of a schoolmaster; "but after you reach the point where you use a split bamboo jointed rod, and a fine rubber reel, it's about time you stepped up a peg, and gave things their right name."

Larry promised to be more careful in the future.

"There, I've got the tangle all out," he said, with a sigh of relief; "and here comes Tony with some bait. What is it you've got? Bully for you, Tony! My! what a nice assortment of fat grubs. I just bet you the bass will grab at 'em like hot cakes. And strange to say, I'm actually feeling a little hungry myself at the thought of supper. Well, here goes for business."

He went to the stern of the boat to cast out. Not just fancying the way the boat happened to lie, Larry picked up the setting pole, and started to push a little. In doing so he happened to thrust the pole into the water. Perhaps he was only trying to see how deep the river was at that point; at least he afterwards declared he had no other idea than that.

Phil, occupied in the little task which he had laid out for himself, paid no particular attention to Larry for several minutes. He was suddenly startled by a shrill screech from his chum. This caused him to leap quickly to his feet; and what he saw was enough to send a thrill through his whole body.

In prodding about with the push pole Larry must have struck some object lying at the bottom of the river, and the sudden appearance of this unsuspected neighbor had given him a terrible shock. It was a tremendous alligator that thrust his snout above the surface, just as Larry, losing his balance, fell into the river with a great splash!

St. George Rathborne

CHAPTER XV

A RIDE ON AN ALLIGATOR

It was certainly a time for prompt action.

Phil Lancing had leaped to his feet at the first cry from his chum. When he saw that tremendous snout thrust up out of the water he felt a thrill. This changed from alarm to horror when unfortunate and clumsy Larry, tripping in his excitement over the side, struck the water with a tremendous splash, not far from the aroused alligator.

During the day just passed Tony had been giving them more or less interesting facts connected with the ugly saurians that had their usual abode in the cypress swamps. Of course, as the lad had been born and raised amid such surroundings, he was familiar with most of the humors of the scaly reptiles; and had himself been engaged in numerous adventures with them in times past.

He had even told with infinite gusto of an occasion where on a dare he had jumped astride the back of a big bull that was caught in a lagoon, and ridden him to and fro for the space of five moments, despite his bellowing and the angry lashing of his active tail.

Naturally, then, these things all seemed to flash before the mind of Phil in that one dreadful second as he stood there, and saw his chum floundering in the river, not ten feet from the ugly teeth of the 'gator.

Larry had somehow managed to seize upon a dangling rope end. It must have been by the merest chance in the world that this came about; but having once clutched this life preserver he held on with a desperate grip.

Meanwhile, he seemed to understand that he was in dangerous closeness to that aroused and angry reptile which his setting pole had prodded. While holding on for dear life Larry was exercising all the agility of a gymnast in a mad effort to do a little rope climbing.

That was where his lack of form told heavily against him. Strive as he would, and spurred on to redoubled labor by a knowledge of his peril, Larry was utterly unable to accomplish what he had set out to perform. Several times he succeeded in drawing himself up a foot or so, and then would come a fatal slip that knocked his plans "galley-west," as Phil would have said.

And at such times Larry was bound to go souse into the stream again, grunting; calling out in half muffled tones; and spouting forth quite a cascade of water that had been taken into his open mouth.

Undoubtedly, had Larry's rescue depended upon himself alone he might have fared badly. He did not seem able to make any headway against the bad run of luck that kept tumbling him back after every effort to rise. And that mossback 'gator, as Tony always called an old fellow, was certainly worked up into a rage which might result in his attacking the struggling boy, despite all his wild floundering

St. George Rathborne

and splashing.

Phil of course suddenly remembered that he had it in his power to assist Larry.

His gun!

If only he could manage to hasten to where it had last been seen, he might yet fire a charge, or several for that matter, full into the eyes of the reptile; and at such a short distance it must surely bring the attack to an end.

While it takes quite some time to narrate these things, in reality it all happened within a few seconds, to tell the truth. Usually Phil was exceedingly active in mind, but somehow the affair seemed to have dazzled him just a trifle, so that he found himself unable to decide just where he had last set eyes on the faithful repeating shotgun.

Larry had even made his second furious attempt to climb up the rope, and fallen back again, when Phil discovered the barrel of the gun sticking out from under a bunch of blankets which his chum had tossed aside in trying to get at his fishing tackle.

Just as Phil was in the act of making a dash for the weapon something flashed by him. It was Tony, the swamp boy; and over his shoulder as he leaped he sent back the words:

"I get him, you watch!"

Nevertheless Phil, being accustomed to depending on himself, did not halt in his dash for the gun. No matter how good the intentions of Tony might be there was always more or less danger that a slip could occur; and in case such a calamity did come about, he, Phil, wanted to be in a position to lend a helping hand.

The dangling rope was in reality the loose end of the painter which Larry had fastened to the trunk of the twisted live oak tree growing near the edge of the bank. As the water was quite deep right up alongside the shore Larry found no footing, and was in his haste making a bad job out of what might otherwise have been easy work.

Afterwards, when he figured matters over, Phil realized that he could not have been more than three seconds in making that frantic dive for the gun, snatching it up in his eager hands, and swinging around once more so that he could have a clear view of the water where this excitement was transpiring. And yet at the time it seemed to him as though an hour must have elapsed, so great was the mental strain.

What he saw caused him to stare as though he could hardly believe his eyes; it was all like a strange dream, this actual realization of the story which Tony had been telling them that afternoon.

The alligator bull was still in sight. He had managed to turn about, so that his ugly snout was pointing directly toward the spot where Larry was still kicking and splashing at a terrific rate in his attempt to be a sailor, and climb a rope, something he had possibly never practiced, the more the pity.

How Tony had ever managed to accomplish it in that very short space of time Phil could never guess; but even as he looked he saw the swamp lad astride the back of the angry 'gator, close up to his head.

The saurian was lashing the water into foam. Perhaps he had just managed to get sight of the struggling Larry, and intended to swim straight for him, had not a new and

St. George Rathborne

unexpected enemy suddenly taken a hand in the game.

Gripping his gun Phil crouched there on the deck of the motor boat, staring at the little swamp boy. Tony was grinning widely as though he delighted in proving in this practical way how true his remarkable story of the afternoon had been.

And looking, Phil saw him lean quickly forward. He seemed to thrust both hands out, with the thumbs turned down, as though seeking the only vulnerable point about that mail-clad head.

"The eyes—he's trying to stick his thumbs in the 'gator's little eyes!" gasped the astounded and thrilled watcher.

He no longer thought of attempting to make use of the weapon he held in his own hands. What was the need when Tony had things all his own way? And holding his very breath with awe Phil Lancing watched the bold play of the swamp boy, who had been accustomed to the ways of alligators from infancy.

"He's done it!" burst from the lips of the one spectator, as a terrific bellow burst from the twelve foot saurian, undoubtedly of pain and rage combined at having his eyes gouged in this fierce manner.

Faster and more violently than ever did that powerful tail thresh the water, until the foam seemed like soap bubbles. Bellow after bellow made the air tremble, or at least pulsate. And amid all this racket the shrill screams of delight on the part of the excited and pleased swamp lad could be heard pealing forth like the notes of a bugle amid the roar of battle.

"Get him up, Phil—get him up!"

It was Tony shouting these words, which brought the watcher to his senses. Why, how silly of him to be crouching there, a mere looker-on, when he ought to be having a hand in the matter.

Thinking thus, Phil immediately sprang away. A couple of bounds took him over the side of the launch and ashore. Here, dropping his now useless gun, he bent down alongside the roots of the live oak, which on this side were exposed to the air by the gradually washing away of the soil.

The first thing Phil saw was the agonized face of his chum. It no longer looked rosy, and beaming with good-nature. Larry was genuinely frightened, and as pale as a ghost. The sight of that terrible monster, which he had unwittingly offended with those prods from his push pole, together with his sudden immersion in the water, had given him a shock.

"Reach up your hand, Larry! I'll give you a pull, and out you come!" Phil cried, as he bent down, and stretched his own willing arm as far down toward the surface of the water as he could.

Larry was only too willing. Indeed, he even let go with both hands, and of course plunged back again into the river, to frantically cry out, and seize once more on the friendly rope-end.

"Careful now! Not so fast, old fellow! Just one hand at a time; and hold on to the rope with the other!" Phil said, encouragingly.

This time, taking warning from his former mishap, and realizing that the more haste the less speed, Larry succeeded in thrusting his left hand into the grasp of the waiting chum above. Phil instantly exerted all his strength; and what with

St. George Rathborne

the frantic efforts of the fat boy, the result was all that could have been wished.

Larry rolled over as soon as he found himself safe on dry land. He gave a grunt of what might be satisfaction; allowed another pint of water to escape; and then, filled with eagerness to witness what strange sights might be transpiring close by, crawled to the edge of the bank again, to stare with dilated eyes at the antics of the swamp boy.

Nor was Phil far behind him in seeking a place where he too might be a witness to Tony's wonderful skill in riding the wild alligator bull.

The baffled saurian, roaring with the pain entailed upon him when the boy thus thrust both thumbs down into his eyes, still lashed the water with his sweeping tail, and had started to swim aimlessly about, unable to see whither he might be heading.

Tony's usually sallow face was aflame with delight. He seemed "dreadfully tickled," as Larry would say over the splendid opportunity to show off before his new Northern friends. They knew all about reading, and the world at large; but neither of them would have dared thus ride a savage bull 'gator. It was surely Tony's hour!

But presently the huge reptile, driven frantic by pain, made a sudden lurch, and dived down into the depths of the river, as though hoping in this way to relieve himself of the terrible enemy that was blinding him.

Amid the foam-crested wavelets Phil saw the swamp boy reappear; and his heart, which had seemingly risen into his throat, resumed its normal beating once more.

"Oh! look, there he is again! Bully for Tony; but didn't he do it fine! Come ashore, Tony, before he gets after you again!" called out the excited Larry.

Tony was leisurely swimming toward them, his face still wearing that broad grin.

"Not much danger he do that, I tell yuh," he answered, coolly. "Old mossback, he get in hole, an' hide a week. Skeer him heap that time. Know him come out o' swamp. Get him hide yet, yuh see if I don't."

Reaching the dangling rope-end Tony climbed up unassisted, scorning the helping hand Phil thrust downward. It was as if he desired to show how differently he might have acted had he been in Larry's place. And that individual immediately made up his mind that after such a humiliating experience he would daily practice such useful stunts as climbing a rope, since there could be no telling when it might come in handy as a life saving exercise.

Tony, upon reaching the top of the bank, shook himself like a big New Foundland dog might have done. He had no coat on at the time, nor had Larry, which proved doubly fortunate, considering their immersion.

And Larry, full of gratitude, insisted on squeezing Tony's hand, while he poured out boyish congratulations on the wonderful feat he had seen the other perform. Tony looked greatly pleased. These two chums had done so much for him that he only too gladly welcomed the opportunity to wipe out a little of the debt.

St. George Rathborne

CHAPTER XVI

UNDER THE TWISTED LIVE OAK

"Where did you ever learn that trick, Tony?" asked Phil, as they once more went aboard the motor boat, Larry to change his clothes before thinking of fishing, and Tony to continue the task at which he had been employed, just as though nothing out of the ordinary had happened to disturb him.

"I tell yuh," replied the swamp boy. "McGee, he one time think he have to get out this part of country and locate 'way down south. Hear lots 'bout Everglades, an' go down coast with sponger on sailboat, tuh see if worth while. I was 'long that trip down tuh gulf; an' McGee, he send me back with other men. But I wanter go 'long an' see them Everglades; hear heap 'bout same from one o' our men. Waited till I get chance, an' crawl 'board sailboat, hide in locker forward. They never find me till I get so hungry second day, have tuh come out."

Phil noticed that Tony seldom referred to the head of the clan as his "father"; it was nearly always "McGee"; just as if he felt more respect for him as the leader of the settlement, than regard for him as his parent.

"I suppose your father was considerably surprised?" he

remarked, smiling.

Tony shrugged his shoulders, as though the memory were not altogether pleasant.

"He was mad clean through," he replied. "He knock me down once, and say he ought to throw me overboard. Then he change his mind, and larf, tellin' me I was a chip o' the same old stick, er somethin' that way. Arter that he act right good, an' I do the cookin' foh the lot. So then we get tuh Everglades. But he never take tuh things down thar like here, an' change mind 'bout leavin'."

"But about the alligator trick, Tony?" asked Larry, who was listening eagerly all me while.

"Come tuh that now, Larry, you see," answered the other, nodding pleasantly. "Meet Injuns down thar. Seminoles they call 'em. Wear shirt, vest, an' a heap o' red stuff wind 'round head; that all. I talk much with Injuns; they tell me how they many times ride on back of big bull. I never hear such thing, an' want'er see, so they take me out in swamp, and one boy he do same."

"Yes," broke in Phil, "I guess you wasn't satisfied to have an Indian beat you in such a trick; and you couldn't rest until you had copied him; isn't that just about right, Tony?"

The swamp boy chuckled as he nodded.

"Reckon I did, Phil," he said, modestly. "Climb on 'gator back while Injun boy thar, push him off, an' keep up game. Never let Injun beat me. But McGee, he shake his head when I tell him, an' look hard at me. Then he larf, an' jest turn 'way."

"I guess he knew there was just no use trying to hold you back, Tony. Say, Larry, are you going to try for fish this evening?" Phil called out.

"I'm ready right now, with some of those nice fat grubs Tony caught me," replied the other, coming out of the boat with dry clothes on.

"Well," continued Phil, "I wanted to say that after all that row here, the chances are you'd never get a bite in a coon's age. If I were you I'd just go up the shore a bit."

"Why up instead of down?" asked Larry, always curious to know the why and wherefore of everything, as a budding lawyer should.

"For one thing, you muddied the water below," Phil went on. "Then again, perhaps you noticed that the old mossback headed downstream; and so the chances are the fish might be scared away for some distance."

"Oh! now I catch on to what you mean, Phil," Larry spoke up. "But you see, there are so many things I don't know about woodcraft, that I've just got to keep asking questions. Then I'll go upstream, and try my luck."

"Be careful not to get out of sight of the boat," warned the other.

Larry looked a bit dubious at these words. He stood there for a minute as if hesitating whether to go or not. But like most boys he disliked to have a chum imagine he were capable of showing the white feather; so presently he sauntered off.

Phil had been observing him out of the corner of his eye, and chuckled a little at noting how loth Larry seemed to be to depart. But Phil did not mean to let the other get out of his sight at this interesting stage of the game. Larry had a weakness for doing just the things he ought to avoid. He could get lost, or fall overboard, or even tumble into a bed of soft ooze, quicker than any one Phil knew.

So, in a few minutes he picked up the gun, and said in a low tone to Tony, who was doing something aboard the boat:

"Guess I'll take a little circuit around for a few minutes. I won't go far; but I want to keep an eye on Larry. He seems to have a weakness for tumbling in; or having something out of the way happen to him. And just now, you know, Tony, when we're so close to your home, I'd hate to have an accident happen to break up all my plans."

Tony did not reply, though he nodded his head to announce that he heard. Perhaps he was a little afraid lest Phil might try to swing around over too large a circuit, and come in contact with some detachment of the shingle-makers from the nearby settlement.

So Phil sauntered off. He realized that there was no excuse for his wandering far, even had the mood been upon him, which was not the case. The going was bad; and with night close at hand it would have been the utmost folly to have started on a reconnoitering trip.

He simply swung around, and then from the rear approached the spot where Larry was engaged in fishing. The other was evidently having some luck, for Phil saw him take one good-sized bass from his hook; and his eager actions would indicate that the finny tribe gave evidence of being hungry.

It was far from Phil's intention to alarm his chum. He simply walked toward him, meaning to speak when he arrived at a

St. George Rathborne

closer point; and then so as not to disturb the fishing; for as an ardent sportsman Phil believed that sounds would carry in the water, and frighten even hungry bass.

He was therefore considerably surprised to see Larry suddenly start up, and dropping his split bamboo rod in a panic, commence running down the bank of the river, showing all the evidences of fright.

Phil glanced hurriedly around. It did not occur at once to him that his own coming must have alarmed the timid Larry; and he half expected to see some gruff swamp squatter heave in sight, as he sent that inquiring look around.

There was nothing near to cause the alarm; not even a bear or a wandering raccoon, so far as he could determine. Then it dawned upon him that Larry must have discovered the apparently stealthy approach he was making, and had naturally suspected that it was some would-be abducter stealing up on him. And Larry seriously objected to being thus carried off.

"Hey! where you going, you Larry?" Phil called out, as soon as he could command his voice for laughing at the ridiculous figure his fat chum presented, sprinting madly along the bank of the stream.

At that Larry slackened his speed, and even condescended to twist his fat neck, so that he could send a look of inquiry back over his shoulder. When he discovered that the supposed kidnapper was only his chum, who seemed to be doubled up with merriment, Larry came to a full stop. Then he started to slowly retrace his trail, shaking his head and grumbling to himself.

"'Twa'n't hardly fair of you, Phil, giving me all that trouble for nothing," he was saying as he drew near, looking a little sheepish because of his recent wild sprint.

"Excuse me, Larry," his chum replied, with becoming regret, though his dancing eyes rather belied his humble tone; "I sure never meant to alarm you one whit. I didn't call out because you seemed to be having a great time with the bass; and sometimes noise stops a biting rally. But I never thought you'd be so keen to get on to me coming along."

"Well, perhaps I wouldn't a while back, Phil, but I'm learning things every day, you see. And besides, didn't you as much as tell me to keep an eye out for any sort of moving thing? That's what I was adoing right now. I saw something creeping along. The shadows are gathering back there under the trees, and I couldn't make out in that one peek what it was. I just cut and run as the safest way."

"And I guess you were right," said Phil. "It might have been a hungry panther wanting to make a meal on you. You know, I always said that if any wild beast was prowling around in search of a supper, he'd pick you out, first pop. That's because you're such a nice, plump morsel."

"Oh, rats! don't make me blush, Phil. Then, if I had to stay down in these diggings long, I'd sure make it a point to lost some weight. It ain't exactly pleasant you see, knowing that even the wild critters are having their mouths water at sight of you. But look at that big bass I yanked in, would you? Must weigh all of six pounds, and enough for our supper alone."

"Did he pull hard?" asked the other, stooping to notice the gasping fish, and to also strike the prize a sharp blow back of the head that immediately killed it; for Phil was a humane disciple of Izaak Walton, and believed in putting even his captures out of suffering immediately, which is a point for all

Boy Scouts to heed.

"Well, for just the first few seconds, yes; and then he seemed to come in like a log, with his big mouth open. Not so much game about him after all. Say, I hope now, Phil, he ain't sick! I'd just hate to have all our supper go to waste that way!"

The other laughed aloud.

"Bless you, Larry!" he exclaimed, "this fish is all right, and as fit to eat as anything. It's just a way they have down here, where the water is always warm. If that same fish had lived in the cold streams up North you'd have had the time of your life getting him ashore with that fine tackle. The climate affects even the native crackers the same way. Where it's warm, and people don't have to hustle just to keep living, they grow lazy. Some people call it the hookworm, you know. My dad often writes articles about it. But to me it seems just pure laziness, and nothing more."

"Now," said Larry, ready for argument at once, as he gathered up his catch, and started down the bank toward the boat, "I just don't agree with you about that business. It ain't just warm weather that makes these crackers shiftless. Take the mountaineers up in West Virginia and Tennessee. They sure get plenty of cold weather most of the year round; and yet they're just like these crackers of the far South. There is a hookworm, as sure as you live. I only hope we don't get it fastened on us while we're down here."

"I see you've been reading up on that subject," remarked Phil. "And some other time we'll get busy again over it. My dad is up on all those subjects and I'm taking some interest myself. But if that's so, then these green trout, as they call the big-mouth bass down here, must have the hookworm bad; for they're just the laziest things I ever saw pulled in."

Tony insisted on taking the catch, and preparing it for cooking; while Larry started up the useful little Jewel stove. Phil would have really kindled a fire under the twisted live oak ashore, only that Tony seemed averse to such a proceeding; and he had promised the swamp boy to avoid doing what was bound to bring the squatters down upon them during the night.

The supper was cooked in detachments. First they had the fried fish, for which the largest frying-pan had to be used. Crackers went well with this; and later on the coffee being boiled, they enjoyed a fragrant cup of Java, together with some cakes that had been put up in air-proof packages, and were as fresh as the day they left the New York bakery.

The night settled down. Clouds had covered the heavens at sundown, and so they had next to no benefit from the moon, though it was evidently mounting some distance above the horizon in the east.

Sitting there later on Phil wondered what the near future held in store for himself and his chum. Would their presence be discovered by the men from the settlement, so that before the coming of dawn they might expect callers; or on the other hand, was it possible for him to carry out his own plan, entering the squatter settlement of his own free will, and demanding to see the terrible McGee, before whom most men had up to this time quailed?

But it was all as mysterious and dark as the night shades gathering there around the motor boat, tied up under the weird twisted live oak.

St. George Rathborne

CHAPTER XVII

TALKING IT OVER

"Listen!"

It was Larry who gave utterance to this exclamation. Phil knew just what his chum must have heard, for several times during the last ten minutes the same sound had been faintly borne to his own ears, though he had not seen fit to mention the fact.

Coming on the night breeze what seemed to be the barking of dogs might be heard. Larry, apparently, did not know whether he could trust to his own judgment.

"Say, ain't that dogs barking, Phil?" he asked.

"Well," replied the other, coolly, "I don't believe they've got any wolves or coyotes down here in Northern Florida; and if they had, we wouldn't be apt to hear them carrying on that way. On the whole, Larry, I guess you'd be safe in calling it dogs, and letting it go at that."

"Poor old Pete!" muttered Larry.

"What's that?" queried his boat-mate, in surprise. "Do you

really think our colored friend Pete is up against it again?"

"Why, he was going to come down this way, you know; and that sheriff seemed so dead set on getting him, that he's chased his dogs all the way," Larry explained.

Phil did not laugh, although he wanted to, for he knew Larry had a lot to learn about the big outdoors, and its myriad tongues.

"Stop and think a bit, Larry," he said, soberly. "In the first place that Sheriff Barker would hardly dare trust himself down here in the McGee country. You remember what Tony told us about how they treated him the last time he was here? And then again, if you notice carefully, you'll find a vast difference between the bay of a hound when on a trail, and the barking of dogs in a settlement."

"Oh! now I catch on to what you mean, Phil!" exclaimed Larry, chuckling. "Then all that racket really comes from the village where Tony's people live; and so we must be pretty close to his home right now."

"That's sound logic, I take it, Larry. How about it, Tony?" asked Phil, turning to the swamp boy, who sat there listening to what was being said, but without saying a word.

"'Bout mile straight across; p'raps two mile round by river," he replied.

"Just about what I thought," Phil went on. "You don't suppose, do you, Tony, they could have heard us when you and Larry were having your jig-time with the old mossback 'gator?"

"Might hear me shout, but b'lieve it other boys," was the

reply which Tony made.

"I'm glad of that," Phil remarked, though he did not explain just why.

"And the more I think about it," Larry spoke up, "the greater I feel that I had a mighty narrow escape. Just you catch me dropping overboard again while we're around this region! Why, Phil, would you believe it, while I was fishing above, didn't I see as many as five of the nasty wigglers go swimming past. Ugh! they give me a cold creep."

"Now what do you mean by wigglers?" demanded his companion.

"Snakes, ugly brown and yellow fellers, with a nasty head, and a wicked look about 'em that I don't like a bit," Larry answered, readily, and shuddering as he spoke.

"Oh! you mean those everlasting water moccasins, do you?" Phil laughed. "Well, they are ugly customers, I admit. And I've heard that their bite is mighty nearly as bad as the rattlesnake's, down here. How about that, Tony?"

"Not so bad, oh, no!" the swamp boy quickly replied. "Sometimes leave sore, not soon heal up. But weuns have medicine tuh take when cotton-mouth or moccasin hit in leg with fangs. We splash when we go through water in swamp, and skeer away. No bother much 'bout moccasin. But rattler more trouble. Two year I get bit, and McGee have much hard time keepin' his Tony."

"I suppose he soaked you with whisky in the good old backwoods way; but Tony, they've got beyond that these days. Doctors have a remedy that will in most cases save the patient, unless he goes too long before being treated."

Phil had himself read up on the subject; but he made no effort to explain to his two friends. Larry would never remember a single thing about it; and the swamp boy of course could not have understood the meaning of much that such an explanation would entail.

All the same Phil was secretly pleased to hear his chum say so decidedly that he did not mean to again allow himself to drop overboard. It would be just like Larry to get bitten in the leg by one of those malignant little snakes, that continually threw themselves into attitudes of defiance on the surface of the dark water, as though ready to give battle to the invaders of their preserves. And in such a case all sorts of trouble might ensue; though Phil's physician father had provided him with the proper remedy to be used under such conditions.

Tony had been so very quiet the whole evening that Phil knew his mind must be taken up with some serious thought.

"What ails you, Tony?" he finally asked, as they still sat there, no one seeming in any hurry to retire on this night. "I wouldn't worry over things, if I were you. Leave matters to me. I'm dead sure I've got that along with me to win over your awful dad, once he learns the truth."

Tony sighed heavily.

"That sound well, Phil," he muttered disconsolately; "yuh mean all right, sure; but yuh don't know McGee! He's gut a terrible temper! Sometimes my mother, even she is 'fraid uh him. Then 'gain, he the kindest man alive. Never know what come. Just like storm, he jump up in summer—one minit sunshine, next howl, and pour down."

"And then it clears up, with the sun shining brighter than

ever, ain't that so, Tony? Of course it is. Well," went on Phil, sagely, "I guess I can size the McGee up, all right. He's just got a fiendish temper. He does things on the spur of the moment, that he's sorry for afterwards. All right. I can understand such a man; and Tony, take it for me, I'd rather deal with such a fiery disposition than the cold, calculating one of the man who never gets mad. I'm going to win over the McGee, see if I don't."

"Huh! just hope yuh do, Phil," said the other, eagerly. "If anybody kin do that, yuh kin, I declar. But I'm 'fraid 'bout what he does w'en he larns that yuh happens tuh be the boy uh Doc Lancing!"

"But Tony, you were thinking about something else too, besides this," the other went on, smilingly.

"Yep, that so, Phil," replied Tony, promptly, as though relieved in a measure to change the conversation to some other subject.

"Was it not about the little sister you left up-river?" Phil continued; for he could read the other like an open book.

"Madge!" murmured the swamp boy, and his soft way of pronouncing that sweet name was the nearest approach to a caress in the human voice Phil had ever heard.

"You're wondering now if the good doctor from the North has arrived on time; and how the operation is going to pan out? Of course you're worried; because you must be anxious to know the best, or the worst. It was a shame that they chased you out of town before he arrived."

"I think so many times," said Tony; "but now I see it not so bad. If I stay thar I never know you an' Larry. It heap worth while that I be 'long with yuh when yuh kim down hyah tuh the land uh the McGee. P'raps Tony might help keep yuh from bein' whipped, er tarred an' feathered."

"Good gracious!" ejaculated poor Larry, as he heard these fearful words drop from the lips of the other; "you don't mean to say he'd think of treating a couple of innocent, harmless kids like that, Tony? But then Phil has a winning way about him; and I'm ready to bank on him to bring your awful dad around."

"How about those pigeons, Tony; do you still believe one of them can get back home, and bring the news your friend expects to send, after the operation has been finished, one way or the other?"

Phil said this for two reasons. He really wanted to know what Tony thought; and at the same time wished to change the conversation; for Larry was apt to dwell upon that ugly black possibility of their feeling the weight of the McGee's violent temper, even though they did not merit the punishment in the least.

"I think they come home," Tony declared steadily. "They fly strong lots times. Of course I never try far 'way, more'n ten mile. Let go then, and always back in coop when I get home. Yep, sure one come with message. Hope it soon, 'case then McGee he mebbe feel not so mad, an' p'raps leave Phil go on down river."

Always was he thinking of his new companions. It gave Phil a strange sensation in the region of his heart to realize how dear he and Larry must have become to this wild son of the swamp, in the brief time he had known them. And on their part, they too felt the keenest interest in Tony McGee and his fortunes.

The hour grew late.

Once in a while some sound would be borne to their ears from the quarter where as they knew by this time the settlement of the shingle-makers lay. The night wind was soft and low, but it carried whispers on its wings. Clouds still covered the heavens, and Phil fancied that they might yet have rain, though there was really no sign of one of those cold storms that periodically come chasing down from the north in winter time, and are termed "Northers" by the shivering crackers.

Larry was beginning to yawn. He did not really want to go to bed as long as the others were up; but tired nature was getting the best of his good intentions. And besides, he had gone through quite a little stress while trying so furiously to climb that rope, so that his muscles were actually sore, though he refrained from telling his chum so, not wishing to be considered in the tenderfoot class any longer.

"Hello! none of that, now!" exclaimed Phil, as upon bending down, after hearing a suspiciously heavy sound of breathing he discovered that Larry had actually fallen asleep while sitting there. "Wake up, and make your bed! The sooner you tumble in, the better for you, old top! Why, you're snoring to beat the band."

"Don't want to go till the rest do," mumbled Larry.

"That's all right," laughed Phil, who could understand the real motive that actuated the now ambitious Boy Scout; "we're all going to follow suit. Hi! get a move on, Tony, and lug out your blanket. No matter what happens, we oughtn't to let it keep us from getting a snooze. That's good horse sense, believe me."

"Sure," said Larry, stirring with an effort, for he felt very stiff. "Me to hit the downy pillow, which ain't so soft after all, if it is made up of only air. But I'm dead tired, and want to rest the worst kind. Thank you, Tony, for helping me. Ain't used to be chased by a moss-back 'gator every day. Kind of gave me a bad five minutes, and I must have taken a little cold too. Now I'm fixed all hunky dory. Good night, fellows! Wake me early, mother dear, for tomorrow—tomorrow—"

Larry did not even finish the sentence. Sleep grappled with his faculties as he was mumbling in this fashion.

"Say, he's off, Tony, as sure as you live," chuckled Phil. "My! don't I sometimes wish I could forget all my troubles like Larry can, as soon as he lays his head down. But no two are alike. And now Tony, that he can't hear us, what's to be the programme in case they come tonight; for I know you more'n half expect to see some of your people turn up here, for Barker will have carried the news home?"

"Yuh jest mustn't do nawthin', Phil," said the swamp boy earnestly. "If so be they comes, weuns has got tuh throw up our hands, and call quits. Take hit jest as cool as yuh kin, an' leave hit tuh me. They ain't agwine tuh hu't yuh, so long's Tony McGee's 'long. An' I sure means tuh let 'em know what all yuh done foh me. Jest hold up yuh han's, and say yuh was acomin' down hyah tuh talk with McGee. An' I reckons as how yuh won't be in too big a hurry tuh tell how yuh happens tuh be Doc. Lancing's boy."

With these last words of Tony's ringing in his ears Phil lay down to try and coax sleep to visit his eyes. But he knew he would have a difficult task, because of the fact that his affairs were now approaching the climax which, viewed from afar had not seemed so serious, but which now took on a more somber hue.

St. George Rathborne

Tony had crawled forward, where he cuddled under his warm blanket. Phil knew that he had taken particular pains to settle himself down, so that he could easily stretch out his hand, and touch the new comrade of whom he had become so fond. It was a mute expression of his devotion; just after the same manner as shown by the favorite hound that curls himself up at his master's feet, where he can be ready to defend him against any ill that springs up unexpectedly.

"Oh! I never wished so much before in all my life," Phil was saying to himself over and over, as he lay there thinking, "that things would turn out all right; and somehow I just seem to feel, deep down in my heart, that they must, they must!"

By degrees his eyes became heavy. He had not enjoyed any too much sleep since the cruise had started. One thing and another had conspired to keep him awake each night; and although Phil was a lad of unusual will power, he had found it beyond him to altogether shut out the possibilities that lay in wait for them in the near future.

Finally he slept.

The night wore on, so that several hours passed. From downstream there came a low sound that was not unlike the dip of paddles. Tony raised his head the better to listen; and from this fact it became evident that the devoted swamp lad had not allowed himself to secure a minute's sleep up to that time.

He listened. Sometimes the sound seemed clear, and then again it would die away, according to the whim of the night air. But Tony was accustomed to judging such things. He presently made up his mind that the dip of paddles was getting continually closer; and that one boat at least was ascending the river, crossing from side to side, as it might be.

Having ascertained this fact to his own satisfaction, Tony reached out his hand, and touched the face of Phil, which was only partly covered by the blanket.

"Yes, what is it, Tony?" whispered the other, arousing instantly, though he had been in a sound slumber at the time.

"They come!" replied the swamp boy, in a tone inaudible five feet away.

Phil was conscious of a sudden thrill of anticipation. No one could say what the immediate future held for himself and his chum. And the discovery of the tied-up motor boat would now be a matter of short duration, once those keen-eyed men from the squatter settlement arrived on the scene.

So Phil only sat there and awaited developments.

CHAPTER XVIII

THE COMING OF THE TERRIBLE MCGEE

The sound of the dripping paddles grew more persistent. Undoubtedly the dugout was drawing closer and closer. Phil could presently distinguish a black moving object ascending the stream; and it was this effort to move against the swift current that caused unusual exertion, and consequent splashing from time to time.

He watched it begin to cross over from the denser shadows along the other bank. Using his eyes to their limit he fancied he could just make out two moving figures in the coming boat. Phil wondered what form their discovery of the object of their search would take; and whether these two fellows might alone attempt to make prisoners of those aboard the motor boat.

All at once he noted that the dark, log-like looking water craft had come to a halt, so far as approaching the bank was concerned. The two men plied their paddles softly now, but only to keep from being carried down-stream by the ever restless current.

They had spied the tied-up craft, and were whispering together. Phil waited to see what they meant to do. If his hand unconsciously crept out toward the faithful Marlin gun, it was hardly with any idea that he meant to make use of the weapon; but instinct alone guided his move.

Ah! now they were once more moving. They had ceased to paddle, and the dugout began to glide down the river. They were apparently going away! Did that mean they expected to pass over the whole two miles between that point and the village of the lawless shingle-makers?

Now he could no longer see them. Tony was stirring again; and Phil believed it safe to send a whisper toward the swamp lad, desirous of seeking information from the one who ought to know.

"They have gone away, Tony!" he said, carefully; but it could not be that he feared arousing Larry, who slept on peacefully through it all, lost to the world.

"Yep, I reckoned they would," came the immediate answer.

"But why did they drop back when they might have climbed aboard, and captured us while we slept?" Phil continued.

"Huh! not gone far. Phil wait, an' see how!"

"Oh! is that it?" echoed the other, as a light began to dawn upon him; and he continued to sit there, watching for a sign.

Perhaps five minutes passed. Phil had no means for marking the flight of time, and doubtless it seemed much more than that to him.

Then he suddenly saw something a little distance down the stream, that told him a fire had been started. Rapidly it grew in volume, until the entire vicinity was brilliantly illuminated; and he could easily see the two squatters moving back and forth, piling brush on the flames.

Of course Phil understood that this was a signal fire. These men, searching all along the river for the mysterious craft that was coming down toward the settlement from the hostile country above, had doubtless arranged to call their fellows to the spot in case they made a discovery.

"It means the coming of the whole bunch, don't it, Tony?" he asked, as he saw the flames shooting upward, so that the light might easily have been seen a mile or more away.

"That so, Phil," replied the other, moodily. "I 'spect this same, yuh know. On'y hope McGee, he be with alluns."

Tony was certainly nervous, which was a queer thing; for ordinarily the swamp boy seemed to be as cool and self-possessed as an Indian brave, who thought it a blur on his manhood to display emotion in the face of his enemies.

Some time passed. The fire was kept burning, though not quite so riotously as in the beginning. Evidently the two men believed that long ere this its reflected light on the clouds overhead must have been seen at the village; and doubtless the entire male population was even now on the way thither, following some strip of dry land that was well known to them.

"There, look, I can count four!" said Phil, with thrilling emphasis.

"Now six!" was the quick response of Tony.

Sure enough, the recruits were arriving very fast. Phil could see them come out of the gloom of the forest, and into the circle of light cast by the fire. All were men, and even at that distance he could mark the fact that they appeared to be of unusual height. But then the people up-river, who hated and feared the shingle-makers of the swamps, had told him they were giants, strapping fellows all.

"Oh! that must be McGee!"

This broke involuntarily from the lips of Phil as he saw a man of even greater stature than any of the others, stride out of the woods, and immediately beckon for the rest to gather around him.

"Yep, it is him!" breathed Tony, who also had his eyes glued on that tall, commanding figure, as though fascinated by its presence, even though he had been familiar with the same from infancy.

Phil was conscious of a queer sensation as he for the first time looked upon the man of whom he had heard so many strange conflicting stories. But long ago he had come to the conclusion that possibly half of the bad things said about the McGee by his enemies could hardly be true. They hated and feared him so much that his faults were undoubtedly magnified many fold; while his virtues remained unsung.

He would see for himself. And judging from the way things were coming on, the crisis could not be long withheld now.

That caused Phil to remember that he had a chum aboard the Aurora. It seemed hardly fair that Larry should be kept in utter ignorance up to the very moment when the mine were sprung. The shock must be all the more severe under such conditions; and Larry would not be saved any agony of mind by the delay.

So Phil leaned over and shook the sleeper.

"Let up on that, Lanky!" grumbled Larry, who had doubtless been dreaming he was once more with some of his comrades at home; "I ain't agoin' to move, I tell yuh. Get breakfast first, and then call me. Go 'way!"

But Phil only renewed his shaking.

"Wake up, Larry!" he called softly; "the shingle-makers have come to board us! Get a move on, can't you?"

A startled exclamation, followed by a great upheaval, told that Larry had now grappled with the truth.

"W—where, which, how, why? Tell me, Phil, what's that fire doing down there? Oh! I hope now they ain't getting it hot for us, the tar, I mean!" he gasped, as he stared in the quarter where all those moving figures could be seen between the blaze and themselves.

"Oh, rats! get that out of your mind, Larry!" observed Phil, though truth to tell, it had cropped up in his own brain more than a few times to give him a bit of worry.

"They begin tuh come this way!" said Tony, with a catch in his voice, as though he were keyed up to a nervous tension because of the situation.

Phil could see this for himself, because there was a general movement among the various figures around the signal fire.

Larry was heard moving restlessly. Perhaps he could not get it out of his mind that the fire had really been started so as to heat up the dreadful tar, with which he and his chum were to be smeared before the squatters made them into uncouth birds by the addition of a shower of feathers, taken from some old broken pillow; and then turned them loose to continue their voyage down-stream.

Yes, the gathered clan of the McGee was certainly marching in the direction of the tied-up motor boat. And at their head came the bulky figure of the giant leader.

Somehow, even in that minute of dreadful uncertainty, Phil was reminded of what he had read about some Highland chief leading his tartan clan to battle, a Rob Roy McGregor, it might be.

But he had to think quickly. Inside of a few minutes the squatters would have arrived alongside the motor boat; and the boys must expect to find themselves virtually prisoners of war; though they had come to this region in Dixie without the slightest hostile intent.

What then?

Phil steadied himself for the great task that he knew awaited him. No doubt he and Larry would be taken across the land to the squatter settlement, so that the women and children might gaze upon them; for something seemed to tell Phil that even now his identity might be known to at least McGee.

"Come, let's light up our lanterns," he said, getting to his feet; "if we're going to have company we oughtn't to receive them in the dark. Larry, you know where to find one; strike a match and give us some light."

He purposely set his chum to doing something, knowing that it was the best way of reassuring Larry. And although the hands of the other trembled more or less as he went about getting the lighted match in touch with the turned-up wick of a lantern, he managed to accomplish the job in a fairly satisfactory manner.

They could hear the muttering of many voices, as the crowd drew near. Evidently the men had noted the springing up of the light, and were wondering whether they would be greeted with a discharge of firearms or not.

If, as most of them doubtless suspected, these people on the boat with whom the son of the McGee seemed to be associating in a queer fashion, were really and truly spies, sent down by their hated enemies above, to find out their weak points so that the sheriff might make the raid he had long threatened, then they might yet be forced to capture the craft by violence; and they were primed for a battle royal.

CHAPTER XIX

TAKEN PRISONER

Both lanterns had now been lighted, and were hung so that the interior of the twenty-four foot motor boat was fairly illuminated. Phil had a fine little searchlight in the bow, which he expected to make use of, if the time ever arrived when they would want to keep moving after nightfall; but there was no necessity for bringing this into play now.

"I only hope none of the vandals think to smash things here, if they carry us away to the village!" Larry gave vent to his thoughts, as they stood and waited for the coming of the squatters.

"McGee, he not let that be, I think," Tony hastened to say, so as to reassure the more timid Larry; who was quivering like a bowl of jelly over the unknown calamities that hung over their heads.

Now the leaders of the marchers were close up. A dozen strong they were pushing forward; and at their head strode the tallest of them all, the man who was head and shoulders above the rest.

"Hello!"

St. George Rathborne

It was Phil who called out, and Larry started as though he had been shot, so strung were his nerves.

The crowd still came on. Perhaps they thought those on the boat meant to put up a desperate resistance; and it was policy in that event for them to be as near as possible, before the word was given to carry the craft by storm.

"McGee, are you there?" continued Phil; and he was really surprised himself at the calm manner in which he could handle his voice; now that the critical moment had really come, all his fears seemed to have vanished.

"That's me!" came back, in the heaviest voice Phil had ever heard; and which in fact seemed to accord perfectly with the giant figure of the head of the clan.

"Come aboard, please," continued the boy, steadily, to the secret admiration of both his chum and Tony. "I've been expecting to drop in at your place tomorrow to see you; but you've beat me out."

"Oh! we has, hey?" growled the giant, as with one effort he jumped upon the boat the curtains of which the boys had drawn up, so that they were fastened to the inside of the standing roof.

Strange to say the first thing McGee did was to reach out and clutch his own boy. But if Phil expected to see him embrace Tony, he was very much mistaken.

On the contrary he shook him much as a dog might a rat, until the boy's teeth seemed to rattle together. But Tony was used to this sort of thing, no doubt; and he would not have protested, even though suffering ten times the amount of pain that may now have racked his slender frame.

"What yuh doin' hyah, boy, tell me that?" roared the big man. "Whar's yuh leetle sister; and why so did yuh desart her up yander? If so be any harm's kim tuh Madge, I'll skin yuh alive, d'ye hyah me?"

Phil was on the point of interfering, but on second thoughts he realized that this was a matter between father and son. Tony could take care of himself; and he knew best how to handle the terrible McGee, whom men so feared.

"She's thar in the horspittal, jest like yuh told me tuh leave her," the boy said, steadily enough. "She's awaitin' till ther eye doctor he kims erlong down from the Nawth. They 'spected him yist'day. Reckons as how he musta arriv."

"But why did yuh kim away, an' leave the pore leetle gal alone thar?" continued McGee, in a low but fearful voice.

Already Phil realized that this man was no common creature, but one to be reckoned with. He could now easily believe the stories he had heard about the tremendous strength of the giant. And it was easy to see how he kept control over the members of the squatter clan by sheer force of character.

"She war bein' looked arter fine. Ther nusses was kind, an' they sez as how nawthin' cud be did till the doctor he kim. But I got chased outen town by a gang o' men, an' they'd sure given me thuh cowhidin' they sez, on'y I hid aboard the boat uh these boys. They be'n mighty good tuh me too. They ain't nawthin' they wouldn't do foh me, I tells yuh. An' ther critter as was leadin' them cowards as chased me acrost kentry, he was Kunnel Brashears!"

Then the shingle-maker broke out into a string of profanity that shocked Larry, and set him to shivering again. He could do little save stare at this remarkable man, and draw in great breaths. No doubt he regretted the evil day he had promised to accompany his chum down into this region of swamps, alligators, wildcats, and lawless squatters. But it was much too late now to think of retreating; they had thrown their hat into the ring, and must accept the consequences of their rashness.

McGee, turning, snatched a lantern from its resting place. This he held alternately in front of, first Phil, and then Larry. Evidently he judged the latter to be of small consequence anyway; for after that moment he paid attention only to the one whom he believed to be the leading spirit in the expedition.

"Yuh don't 'pear tuh be a Southerner?" he said, frowning at Phil.

"Oh! no, I've only come down here with my friend for a trip. We had the boat sent by rail, and launched her in the river above here. We expect later to run on down to the gulf, and do some cruising there. But first of all I wanted to stop over with the shingle-makers of the swamps, and meet you, McGee!"

Phil said this without putting on airs. He knew that any one who found himself virtually in the power of these independent people, who recognized no law save that of might, would be exceedingly foolish to show signs of boasting. It was man to man now, and money did not count in the comparison.

"Yuh wanted tuh meet up with me, yuh say?" the other observed, with sarcasm in his tones. "Wall now yuh see me, p'raps yuh don't jest like my looks. If so be I thort them coward hounds up-river sent yuh down hyah tuh spy on us, an' inform thet rail-rid sheriff how he cud git tuh cotch us on the sly, I'd jest lay a cowhide acrost yer backs till the welts they stood up like ropes."

"I have nothing to do with the people of that town," declared Phil, resolutely. "So far as I saw of their actions, they are a lot of cowards, who could chase after a half-grown boy, but draw the line at coming down here to meet men."

"Then tell me why did yuh pick out this yer stream tuh bring yer boat down; I reckons they be heaps o' others thet'd suited better?" demanded McGee.

"Why, I told you that I wanted to see you and that it was with that plan in my mind I selected this river of them all," replied the boy.

Tony was hovering near. He had not even attempted to escape when that iron hand of his father loosened its clutch on his shirt. Of course he understood to what end all these things must lead; and that it was now a mere matter of seconds when the fact must be disclosed that the boy with whom he had been associating was in reality the only son and child of the man these squatters hated above every human being on earth.

And he could imagine the effect of that explosion on the hot temper of McGee. No wonder then that Tony felt alternate flushes of heat, and spasms of cold pass over his body, as he hung upon every word Phil gave utterance to. He dreaded what his father might be tempted to do in the first flash of his anger; and Tony was holding himself ready to jump into the breach. He was accustomed to feeling the weight of the McGee's displeasure, but it pained him to think that it must fall on his best of benefactors, and his new found chum.

The man again flirted the lantern forward, as he took another

St. George Rathborne

look into the calm face of the boy. Phil met the piercing gaze of McGee with a steadiness that doubtless impressed him; for of a certainty McGee must be a reader of character, since he had never had a school education.

He knew that this was no ordinary young fellow who had come down the river on board the new-fangled boat that needed nothing in the way of oars, yet made no steam like the tugs which came up to take their cypress shingles to market.

A number of the men had climbed aboard by this time. They stood around, staring at the elegance to which they were unaccustomed; yet not venturing to so much as lift a finger toward taking possession of things. Until their leader gave the word they would refrain from looting the captured boat. His simple word was law among the swamp shingle-makers.

"Yuh keep asayin' as how yuh wanted tuh meet up wid me, younker," McGee presently remarked in his deep, booming voice. "Wall, now, surpose yuh jest up an' tells why yuh shud feel thetaway. If harf they sez 'bout the McGee be true, they ain't nobody but a crazy men as'd want tuh run acrost 'im."

"But I don't believe one-half of what I hear about you," said Phil. "They warned me that it was foolish to make the try; but I kept on saying that McGee was a fighter who never made war on boys, and he'd listen to what I had to say, even if he didn't want to shake hands, and call it a go."

"What's thet?" demanded the giant, suspiciously. "Yuh act like yuh kerried sumthin' 'long wid yuh, younker?"

"So I do—a message, a letter to you, McGee!" came the quick reply.

"Then yuh'll jest hev tuh deliver it in tork, 'case I cain't read a word. My wife, she allers wanted me tuh larn; but I sez as how 'twar no use tuh me in my line o' work; so she gets the chillen tuh take hit up. Tony thar kin read; an' the lettle gal she knows heaps foh a blind chile. But speak up, younker, an' tell me who sent yuh wid the letter?"

"My father did, McGee," Phil went on, striving to keep the tremor from his voice. "He believed that you had been deceived about him, and he was determined that you should know him as he is, not as he has been described to you by those who want to make trouble."

"Yuh father? Tell me, who's boy be yuh?" demanded the giant, scowling ominously as he bent down over the young owner of the power boat.

"His name is well known to you," said Phil, boldly; "it is Doctor Gideon Lancing, of Philadelphia."

CHAPTER XX

AMONG THE SHINGLE-MAKERS

At first Phil thought the giant was about to strike him a frightful blow; for the hand that was free from holding the lantern doubled up fiercely. Tony, indeed, uttered a pitiful little cry that was almost a sob; and throwing himself forward clung to the arm of his terrible father. But he was immediately flung roughly aside as though he were but vermin.

"So, yuh be his boy, ther man as is a-gwine tuh cla'r weuns off his land if hit takes all ther sojers in Floridy tuh do hit?" gritted McGee between his strong white teeth.

Then his mood seemed to change like magic, for he laughed hoarsely, and looked around at the rough spirits by whom they were hemmed in.

"Wot yuh think o' thet, men, this hyah leetle critter is the son o' ole Doc. Lancing, ther man we's gwine tuh tar an' feather jest as soon as he dars show his hide down thisaways. He jest kim hyah as trustin' as a dove, thinkin' weuns'd never dar lift a hand ag'in 'im, case the sojers they'd foller arter him. Wot we'll jest do tuh this kid ain't wuth mentionin', air hit, men?"

Then arose loud and tumultuous shouts, that made poor Larry crumple up as if he wanted to hide in a thimble. He looked around at the dark and angry faces to the right and to the left; and again wished he had thought twice before embarking on this wild scheme of Phil's.

"Shut up!" roared McGee; and the tumult was hushed as if by magic.

The leader looked about him, his strong face working with mingled passion and pleasure. Phil was somehow reminded of a story, heard in the long ago, a parable about the lord of the vineyard, who sent his son to treat with those in possession; and what those unruly spirits did to the young man was so vividly impressed on his mind right now, that it gave him a very uncomfortable feeling. History might repeat itself. And he was the son of the rich man who owned the property!

"Listen tuh me, men," called out McGee, when every eye was glued on his face. "We'll take these critters back tuh hum with us. Ben, let Marty hev yuh gun. I 'p'int him tuh stay by the boat, and guard thuh same. An' remember, all o' yuh, if so much as a single thing is stolen, yuh'll give an account tuh McGee! understan'?"

Evidently they did, for a number of faces assumed a look of disappointment, as though hopes had been entertained that they were to loot the motor boat, just as though they were pirates of the Spanish Main.

"Git ashore, you!" said the giant, as he motioned with his hand after the manner of one who was accustomed to being obeyed.

Phil did not even attempt to pick up his gun. He knew that weapon would be of no use to him in his present trouble.

Something far stronger than a repeating shotgun was needed to extricate him from the difficulty into which his venturesome spirit had carried him.

Still, he was far from being discouraged. He had not yet shot his bolt. When this leader of the shingle-makers learned about the magnificent offer which his father had made, surely he could never hold the same feelings of bitter resentment and hatred toward the new owner of all those miles of cypress swamps, with their millions upon millions of feet of valuable timber waiting to be marketed.

"Come on, Larry, we're going to see the village of the McGees sooner than we expected," and as he stepped from the boat to the shore, Phil took care to link his arm with that of his chum, being desirous of cheering the other up as well as possible.

"And do we have to walk two miles over all that ricketty kind of land?" groaned poor fat Larry, perspiring at the very thought of the labor.

So they left the motor boat, and Phil could not help wondering whether they were fated to ever set eyes on it again. Perhaps the men might disregard the orders of their chief, and loot the craft of everything movable, even disabling the steady going motor, so that it would be as so much waste junk afterwards.

Tony must have divined his thoughts, for he took occasion to run alongside, and mutter in Phil's ear:

"Don't yuh bother 'bout the boat; she won't be teched arter what he sed. Ther man don't live thet dar's go ag'in McGee's order. Hit's all right, Phil, all right!"

They quickly reached the spot where the big signal fire had burned long enough to bring the crowd all the way from the distant village. It was still blazing up now and then, so that the near vicinity was far from gloomy; but the work of the fire had been finished.

McGee led the way straight to where the long hollowed-out log boat rested, the prow drawn up on the shelving shore.

"Git in!" he said, in his deep voice that was like the rumble of distant thunder.

"Bully! we're going to paddle down by water! Ain't I glad though!" exclaimed the relieved Larry, as he only too gladly clambered over the edge, and found a seat amidships of the dugout canoe.

"Yuh git in too, Tony," said McGee, gloomily, as he motioned to his boy.

Evidently he was still in a towering rage but at the same time there were so many things he could not understand in connection with the coming of this Lancing boy, and Tony's being in his company, that he was holding himself back with a great effort.

McGee himself sat in the stern of the boat, paddle in hand. As they expected to drift with the current, always swift in these deep Florida streams, there was no need of additional motive power; though Tony had also picked up another paddle, as if he meant to assist.

So they started away. Looking back Larry could for some time see the lanterns gleaming aboard the snug motor boat, and how his heart went out to the cozy little craft. If only he and Phil were again aboard, and many miles below this settlement of the lawless shingle-makers, how delighted he would be. He even gave a deep sigh that was akin to a groan when a turn of the river blotted out the glow of those twin lights, and darkness profound surrounded them.

There was only the mysterious gurgling of the black water, or the measured dip of the paddle, with its consequent dripping of unseen drops, to tell that they were speeding swiftly along; though if he looked shoreward Larry could see the bordering trees passing in solemn review, and in this fashion might realize just how fast they were progressing.

No one said a word during the little voyage. Phil was busy with his own thoughts, and arranging his programme for the expected interview with McGee, when he meant to spring his surprise on the gruff giant. Larry on his part had apparently lost all inclination to speak; which was something quite out of the common with him, since he liked to hear himself talk, and believed that a budding lawyer should always find something to say.

Tony was dumb with a nameless fear. He knew the violent rage into which this father of his could fly, and he dreaded lest while in such a state McGee do that which he might always regret. And the giant in turn was puzzling his brain with the intricacies of the problem by which he was faced.

Larry felt a hand twitch his arm.

"Look ahead," said the voice of his chum in his ear; and upon raising his head, and casting his eyes beyond the prow of the long dugout, he discovered lights.

"The village!" he exclaimed; but it would be hard to discover anything like pleasure in the quavering voice with which he said this.

"Thet's it!" observed Tony, listlessly.

McGee made no remark, but continued to ply the paddle. Presently the boat was headed in toward the shore. Phil saw that it would have been next to impossible for the Aurora to have passed by here without being discovered; unless they had picked out an hour between midnight and dawn, when all the settlement might be asleep.

As the boat ran up on a shelving beach, Tony was the first one to jump out. In rapid succession Phil, Larry, and finally McGee himself, stood on the shore.

Their coming had been already noted. Several yellow mongrel dogs came bounding toward them, barking loudly; but at one word in the heavy voice of McGee it was astonishing to see how quickly they cowed down, and with tails between their legs, skulked away.

"Why, even the dogs fear him like the devil does holy water!" whispered Larry, in the ear of his chum.

"He's a wonder, that's what!" muttered Phil; for despite the apparent violent nature of the big man, there was something attractive about McGee; and Phil really believed that once he gained the good will of the other, the squatter head of the clan would prove to be a different sort of a man from what rumor pictured him.

After the dogs came a swarm of dirty children of all ages. Many were in rags, all of them barefooted, and the girls had unkempt hair that made them look all the wilder.

Evidently when the light had been seen, and the men went forth in obedience to the signal, the balance of the inhabitants of the village had been aroused, and remained up ever since, waiting to see what would be the result.

Somehow Phil felt deeply stirred at seeing how poverty stricken the women and children were. Money must be a scarce thing among them these days. Perhaps it was the fault of the men, who would work only when the humor seized them; or again it might be that they got such a small price for their shingles by the time they reached market that it was only with difficulty they kept the wolf from the door.

And yet these wretched people cared for their homes here in the midst of the great swamps; yes, so much so that they were ready to fight for them, wretched hovels that they seemed to be in Phil Lancing's eyes.

Wondering looks were cast upon the two boys as they followed McGee up the bank, and into the midst of the village. Perhaps they might even have been a target for more or less abuse only that McGee was along. When some of the boys began to call out, and thrust their hands toward Larry, as if threatening to pinch him, because he was so very plump, the giant only needed to turn and glare at the offenders to make them slink away, thoroughly cowed.

Several old men seemed to be the only ones about the place, all of the others having hastened to obey the signal when McGee led off.

"And all this can be changed, if only he will accept the generous offer I am bearing him," said Phil to himself, as he looked around at the evidences of squalor and poverty. "Inside of six months this place could have a thrifty look; the women would own decent dresses, the children shoes for their feet if they wanted them; yes, and even a schoolhouse would stand right in the middle of the village, with a teacher ready to show these poor things how to read and write, if nothing more. Oh! don't I hope he acts sensible, and accepts! But I'm more afraid than I'd like Larry to know. I can see a lurking look in McGee's eyes that frightens me, even while I'm smiling so bravely."

He had just finished saying this to himself when he saw Tony leading a woman toward them. There was something akin to pride in the action of the swamp boy.

"It's his mother, Larry," said Phil, instantly; "don't you remember that he told us long ago she used to teach school down in Pensacola, or somewhere else?"

"Well, you'd hardly believe it now," muttered Larry; for the woman was very much like the others of the squatter village, in that her dress was homely.

But Phil noticed that her hair was neatly arranged; and despite her coarse attire there was a certain air of refinement about her.

Tony had evidently managed to give her an inkling, not only as to the identity of his new friends, but how they had been so good to him. She was smiling as she advanced, even though Phil could also see a shadow of anxiety on her face.

"She ought to know the McGee, if anybody does," he thought. "And she is afraid he'll be mean toward us, and think only of striking a blow at the man he has come to hate without any real cause."

It was not a pleasant thought, and Phil tried hard to get it out of his mind by advancing to meet Tony and his mother. McGee, as if convinced that escape was utterly impossible, did not seem to pay much attention to his prisoners, once he had brought them safely to the village. He was talking to the two old men, and probably telling them just who Phil was, for they could be seen scowling as they glanced toward the boy.

"This is him, mother," said Tony, pointing to Phil, whose hand he hastened to grip.

Phil saw the eyes of the wife of McGee survey him closely. Perhaps she had half expected to see some sort of wild animal; for surely such a stern, cold-blooded tyrant as Doctor Lancing had been pictured to these ignorant people of the swamp lands he owned, could only have a son of like character. But if so her disappointment was complete.

"I am glad to meet you, Philip," she said, in a soft, Southern voice, and with all the refining influences about it that years among these strange people could not banish. "My son Tony tells me you have been very kind to him. I only wish I could say I was glad you have come; but my husband has conceived a most dreadful feeling toward your father; and I am afraid it will fall heavily upon you. All that I may do to soften his anger you can count on; but I fear it will not be of much avail, when once his temper is aroused."

Phil pressed her hand with great pleasure. He saw that despite her constant association with such demoralizing influences, Mrs. McGee was still a true Southern gentlewoman. And as a morsel of yeast may leaven the entire lump of dough, so her presence here in the midst of such unruly elements might yet prove their salvation.

"Oh! I'm not afraid, ma'am, I promise you," he replied, laughing as he spoke; although he really did not feel one-half so merry as he made out; for he could see the baleful eyes of the watching McGee fastened upon them at that minute, as he stood not far away. "I came here on purpose to meet

McGee. I carry a letter from my father, in which he asks the assistance of every man in this place to build up a lumber business here on the river, and market the stuff at top-notch prices. It would mean money right along for every worker; it would mean that each family might have a patch of land all their own, as big as they could work for a garden; and it would mean that from this time on the women of this place would be able to have the things they should. I am telling you this, ma'am, so you can carry it to the other women; because, perhaps in the end, we may have to depend on their influence to swing the men around. And that is the message my father sends. He wants to be the friend of you all; and he's coming down here himself to prove that his letter stands for the truth!"

And as the poor woman saw the brightness of the picture he painted tears came unbidden into her eyes, and she turned hastily away to hide her emotion.

CHAPTER XXI

A GLOOMY OUTLOOK

"What can we do, Phil?"

As Larry put this question he looked mournfully at his chum, and tried to keep from shivering, though it was indeed hard work.

The night had passed. Both boys had been allowed a chance to secure some sleep, having been placed in an empty shanty; but as neither of them dared lie down on the straw that formed a rude couch on the board floor, they were compelled to "snatch a few winks," as Larry termed it, sitting up.

In the morning they had been fed, after a fashion. Larry bemoaned the fact that while he had to partake of the unsavory mess or go hungry, all that fine "grub" was going to waste on the Aurora, not more than a mile away.

Phil did not show the anxiety he felt. Since coming into personal contact with the terrible McGee he had lost some of the enthusiasm and confidence that had up to then marked his actions. The leader of the squatter clan was so much more formidable than he had anticipated, that Phil himself began to fear his mission was doomed to be a failure.

It was a serious outlook they faced, particularly Phil. They might allow Larry to get off scot free, since he was not a Lancing, and looked so innocent of any wrong intent; but with Phil the matter was different.

What if the stubborn giant utterly refused to believe the good intentions of the new owner of the cypress swamp lands? What if he felt convinced that it was all a sly trick; and that the millionaire had sent his son down simply to take notes, in order that presently the sheriff, backed by the State troops, could enforce the edict of eviction?

Phil always put that idea away from his mind when it tried to force itself upon him. And yet from every hand he had heard that McGee was a most determined man, who, having conceived a thing, could not be changed. Even his own wife and son had said that about him.

And so, still hoping for the best, Phil now turned toward his troubled chum, with a forced smile on his face.

"Nothing much, I guess, Larry; only wait for a chance to talk again with McGee," he replied, cheerily.

"But the morning is passing, and he doesn't seem to want to see you at all," complained the other.

"But sooner or later he will, you mark me," answered the positive one, wishing to ease the strain he knew was on Larry's poor mind.

"But you told his wife what sort of message you carried," Larry went on, his voice dejected enough to imagine him at a funeral; "and sure she must have managed to let him know, because she promised to do all she could."

"That's what I'm banking on," Phil continued. "She must have more or less influence with McGee. He is proud of her education; and wants his children to follow after her, and not be raised as ignorant as himself. So perhaps the leaven in the lump will work. Only when he gets one of his pig-headed streaks on, nobody in the world can influence him, Tony admits."

"Poor Tony looked so mournful when he brought in our breakfast; I felt bluer than ever just to see him," remarked Larry.

"Yes, the boy is really fond of us," Phil declared, with conviction in his tone. "He can see further than his obstinate dad, and knows the golden opportunity for a future is now in the grasp of McGee. He dreads the result of passion blinding his father to everything else."

"So do I," asserted Larry, briskly. "I can't help thinking of what Tony said about making that sheriff into a bird! What if they take a notion to do us that way. Just imagine me with a nasty, sticky coat of black tar; and then covered with downy feathers! Oh, my goodness! Phil, however would I get it off again? Every inch of skin would come with it."

"Well, don't get cold feet, Larry, whatever you do," remarked his chum; though the gruesome picture Larry drew made him shut his teeth hard together, and turn a trifle pale. "I'm in hopes that, no matter what they do to me, they'll let you off, because you're not concerned in this matter at all."

"Ain't I?" cried Larry, indignantly. "I'm your chum, I guess; and what's good enough for you is ditto for me. If they hand you a new coat, think I'm going to let 'em skip me in the bargain sale? Not for Joseph! Not for a minute! Sink or swim, survive or perish, we're pards, you and me, Phil. If you can stand it, sure I ought to; and that's flat!"

Phil stretched out his hand, and squeezed that of his comrade. At any rate it was worth something just to learn how loyal a chum he had; though perhaps he might have fancied some other way of ascertaining the fact.

"Seems to me there's a whole lot of excitement going on outside there!" remarked Larry, suspiciously, some time later. "And I'm going to try and see if I c'n get a squint at the same. Perhaps this is a holiday for the McGees. Perhaps they're bent on having high jinks because they expect to feast on that nice supply of civilized grub in our motor boat. Oh! won't I just be glad if ever we get back to decent living again. Hoe cake baked in ashes may be filling; but it don't strike me just in the right spot; and especially after I've seen the old woman who cooked it, too. Ugh!"

Grumbling in this fashion Larry proceeded to climb up to the little window that seemed to be at some distance from the floor; and which made Phil believe this particular shanty must have originally been intended for a prison of some sort.

A minute later a loud exclamation and lament from Larry drew his attention.

"What's all the row?" he demanded, his own curiosity aroused.

"Oh! if you could only see what they're doing, Phil?" groaned the clinging one, as he still stared out of the small opening through which the outside air reached the captives of the squatter tribe.

"Suppose you tell me, then?" suggested Phil, promptly enough.

"Don't you believe these shingle-makers down here may have just a little touch of Injun blood in their veins?" demanded Larry. "Because, as sure as anything, they're driving two big stakes right into the ground out here—two of 'em, do you understand, Phil? And the kids are a-dancin' around like the very old Harry; just like Injuns might do when they expected to burn a prisoner at the stake!"

"What!" cried Phil, staggered at first; and then incredulous at the strange assertion of his chum, he too started to climb up the rough log wall so as to reach the window opening.

"There, look for yourself, Chum Phil!" gasped Larry, as the other joined him. "I just felt it in my bones I would come to some bad end. But, oh! what would my poor mother think if she knew her boy was going to be a candle, a torch!"

"Oh, shucks! Larry, don't you believe that sort of stuff!" Phil declared, even though it did look very significant to see those twin stakes being driven into the ground, with a crowd of ragged and barefooted youngsters showing savage delight, as keen as though a circus had come to town.

"Then what are they meaning to do with those stakes?" demanded Larry.

"Oh! well, that's hard to say," stammered Phil. "Perhaps they do expect to fix us up there, just for a frolic, and have some fun with us. But even McGee, ugly as he is, wouldn't dream of burning anybody at the stake!"

"All right then, it's the other thing," said Larry. "Just look at what they're luggin' over now, and tell me if you can, what it is."

When the industrious bunch of half-grown boys opened up

enough for Phil to get a glimpse of the heavy object that engaged their attention, he could not keep from uttering an exclamation of chagrin.

"See, you know just as well as I do that it's a sure melting pot for tar!" exclaimed Larry, hoarsely. "Anybody with one eye could see that, because there's tar all over it. Guess they use it with some of their boats. And Phil, look at that old hag toting that awful bag on her head. What d'ye suppose is in that but geese feathers as old as the hills! Oh, murder! we're up against it good and hard. I can almost feel my wings beginning to sprout right now!"

"Hold on, Larry," Phil remarked. "It looks like they meant to scare us, and have a little fun at our expense; but that doesn't mean they'll go through the whole performance. Give me a chance to spring my father's letter on McGee, and see what it does to him. Why, he would have to be next door to crazy to refuse such a magnificent offer to go into partnership with the man who owns these lands; for that's about what it means in the end."

"But they say he is nigh crazy when he gets one of his stubborn fits on!" declared the other, dejectedly. "He just can't see anything else but the one thing that's on his mind. And right now, Phil, that's the fact of his having in his power the only son of the man he hates like poison. Besides, you told me he said he couldn't read a word; so how's he goin' to know that the letter says what you declare it does?"

Phil had himself thought of that.

"His wife could read it for him, or perhaps even Tony," he said.

"Aw! d'ye think a suspicious man like McGee would trust

St. George Rathborne

either of 'em in a matter like this? Not for a minute, Phil. He'd think they might be fooling him, just to save us from getting our downy coats. Try something else, please."

"Tony said there was one old fellow in the settlement who could read," observed Phil, thoughtfully. "Don't you remember he told us a queer story about old Daddy Mixer, who seems to be some sort of natural doctor among these people, and comes by his name from mixing all sorts of herbs as medicine. He can read; and besides, McGee would believe him where he mightn't his own family."

"Say, that's so!" exclaimed Larry, looking decidedly interested. "And you could ask to have him read it out loud, so everybody might hear the generous offer your good dad makes to every man, woman and child now living on his lands down here. Oh! perhaps it might sweep the crowd off their feet. Don't I hope now it does that same thing. I ain't yearning for a new suit of down one little bit."

"It may please the ragtag and bobtail crowd from the ground up," said Phil soberly; "but you take it from me, Larry, unless McGee himself is convinced, there's nothing doing. He's the Great Mogul of this place, the PooBah of the swamp settlement. When he takes snuff they all sneeze. He holds all the offices; and not a man-jack of them dares to say a word, when McGee holds up his finger. He rules with a rod of iron. So it is McGee alone I'm hoping to convince. That done, the others will fall in line, just like knocking down a row of bricks."

"There he is now, with a lot of the men around him. They keep looking over this way, Phil, like they were talking about us."

"And I guess that's what they're doing," remarked the other, as he watched the gesticulating group a minute. "I wonder, now, has Tony's mother spread the news far and wide among the other women of the village? What if they've already scented the glorious chance to get the things they've just wanted all their lives? And each woman may have been laying down the law to her man! Yes, they seem to be arguing about something or other, for most of 'em look sour or disgruntled."

"But just notice McGee, would you?" sighed Larry. "He looks as black as thunder when he speaks first to one and then to another. They're dead afraid of him, that's what! They've had their say, and he's put a damper on it all. See him shake his fist at that fellow; and how he cringes like a whipped cur! Oh! Phil, whatever did you come down here to try and do anything for that terrible tyrant?"

But Phil shook his head, as though not yet wholly convinced that he had made a serious blunder in undertaking the trip.

"There is a heap of good in that man," he declared between his set teeth; "if only one could get under his tough hide. I'm still hoping the letter will strike home with him, Larry. Don't lose all hope yet!"

"But if it doesn't, we're in a bad box, Phil," said Larry, despairingly.

"Looks like it," Phil admitted, grimly. "But anyhow, we're not going to be kept in suspense long, for he's sending a couple of fellows this way; and it must be they mean to take us out."

Larry drew a long breath, and slipped down from his perch, looking very pale.

St. George Rathborne

CHAPTER XXII

PHIL SHOOTS HIS BOLT—AND LOSES!

The door of the shanty opened presently, and the two squatters stood there.

"Yer tuh kim out, kids; McGee wants yuh!" said one of the pair of brawny shingle-makers beckoning with his finger.

Phil was eagerly scanning their faces. He wanted to know whether his theory of the actual conditions existing in the squatter village might be founded on facts. And from what he saw he believed that it was even so.

Both men looked anything but hostile, as they faced the prisoners. Indeed, unless Phil was very much mistaken, he could detect even a gleam of friendliness in the countenance of the fellow who had spoken.

"McGee's wife has spread the story among the women," he thought; "and it has taken with them like wildfire. In turn they have talked with their men about the wonderful things that would happen, if they chose to change their ways of living, and accepted my father's offer to get steady jobs, and land of their very own. But unless he falls in with the scheme, it's all wasted. They just don't dare call their souls their own down here. And a mutiny is the last thing they'd ever think of starting. Still, when a woman makes up her mind, sometimes she'll find a way to do things."

In this fashion then he tried to bolster up his slipping courage, as he fell in behind the two men, and marched out of the shanty prison. Larry trotted along in the rear; for Phil purposely refrained from slipping his arm in that of his chum; wishing to make it appear that Larry at least was innocent of wrongdoing, and should not be made to suffer.

Had the other boy dreamed that this was his reason for preceding him he would never have allowed it; but so many things were knocking at Larry's brain door he just could not grasp the situation fully, and believed that Phil might have for the minute forgotten all about him.

There was a hush as the two boys came into view. Every eye seemed to be turned toward them; and Phil felt positive that the entire population of Swamptown must be congregated there in the center of the place—men, women and children, down to the babes in arms.

A motley crowd they seemed; and yet not a hostile one, he believed, as he swept a hungry glance around—an anxious look, born of extremity.

The men in the main looked rather hangdog, as though ashamed of the part they must play in the affair, because of their domination by the savage McGee giant. As for the slatternly women, Phil really believed he could see lines of worry on many faces; as if they feared that the best chance that had ever come their way were fated to be cast aside, just through the obstinacy of one man, and he the McGee.

The younger element alone appeared to look upon the

St. George Rathborne

occasion as a picnic especially arranged for their benefit. They grinned, and nudged each other, and seemed ready to back the leader up in any desperate plan he might see fit to carry out.

McGee stood there, with his arms folded across his massive chest. As he drew closer to the giant Phil wondered after all whether he might not have injured his cause by thus setting the balance of the camp against the man who had been leader all these years, by virtue of his brute strength, and his commanding ways.

McGee looked at him with a black scowl on his heavy face. His wife and Tony were near by, both of them white-faced and anxious; as though fearful lest after all the man's natural obstinacy was about to bring ruin upon their newborn hopes.

Phil stood directly in front of the big man. He tried to meet his piercing gaze frankly and steadily, yet not arouse his passion further by a display of bravado.

As for Larry, he kept as near his chum as possible, listening, and hoping for good news, yet fearing the worst. Every time his eyes were drawn toward the twin stakes, against his will as it seemed, he would shudder, and shut his teeth hard together, as though suffering dreadfully. Yet Larry was inwardly determined not to show the white feather if he could help it.

"Younker," said McGee, in his deep voice that seemed so in keeping with his tremendous physique; "yuh admits as how yer the boy uh Doc. Lancing, don't yuh?"

"Why, yes," Phil replied, as pleasantly as he could, yet with firmness. "I told you right in the start that was a fact; and also why I had chosen to voyage down this river instead of choosing the Suwanee. It was to meet you, McGee; to shake hands with you; and let you see a letter my father had given to me. I told you I came in peace, and with a white flag of truce; I said my father wanted to be the friend of every man, woman and child on these lands; and was ready to enter into a contract with you all, binding himself to almost your own terms. That's why I'm here, McGee. That's why I made no attempt to run when you and your men came. I expected that you would treat me just as messengers are always treated in war times, when they come under the white flag of truce."

"An' yuh sped me tuh believe all thet?" demanded the giant.

"I hoped you would, McGee," replied Phil. "We helped your boy Tony before we even knew that he was a McGee; and after we found it out, it made us like him all the more. My father wants you to be his friend, to enter into a new arrangement that will mean plenty of money for you all, and homes that the law can never take away from you. It means the highest wages paid in the lumber business to every man willing to work with him. He wants to develop this country, and knows he can only do it with your help. McGee, here is my father's letter! Won't you have it read out loud, so everybody can hear what a fine man Doctor Lancing really is?"

McGee gingerly accepted the missive Phil took from an inner pocket. His face was still as black as a thundercloud. He had heard the low murmurs of approval that sprang from the lips of some of those near by, possibly the women, who were not quite as much in fear of the lord of the squatter camp as the men. And it angered McGee to think that his authority was questioned in the least.

"Yuh knows right well, younker, as how I cain't read!" he declared.

"Then let some one else read it out—perhaps your wife?" suggested Phil, eagerly.

The giant looked toward his wife, and she even started toward him, only too anxious to accept the opportunity; but with a sneer on his face he waved her back.

"Not on yer life, Molly," he snapped. "I knows wot yuh ben talkin' 'bout lately. Yuh wudn't stop at deceivin' yuh husband one minit. Nor yuh either, Tony. Yuh gotter eatin' the bread uh Doc. Lancing on board thet gimcrack boat, an' ain't tuh be depended on."

He looked around, and then beckoned to an old, decrepit fellow, whom Phil realized must be the "medicine man" of the colony, Daddy Mixer.

"Kim hyar, Daddy," said McGee, with a curt nod; and the old fellow hastened to obey, only too eager to find favor in the sight of the ruler. "Take this hyar paper, an' look her over. Tell me wot hit sez, d'ye mind, an' on'y that, if yuh know wots good foh yuh, Daddy."

The wizened-up specimen of an ague-shaken squatter took the letter in a hand that trembled; and his eyes eagerly passed over the same. It was fortunately done on a typewriter, so that the sentences were as clear as print; and at the end was signed the name of Doctor Gideon Lancing.

"Kin yuh read it?" demanded McGee, grimly.

"I a'ready done it," replied the old man; who had possibly long years ago been given the chance for a schooling.

"An' does hit state jest wot the younker sed?" went on the giant; while Phil and Larry and all within hearing hung on his words.

"It does jest that, McGee. It tells as how the writer he wants ter hold out the olive branch o' peace to the settlers on his lands. He goes on to say as how he offers every fambly an acre, or as much more as they wants, for ther really own, the deed to the same to be delivered over to 'em without a cent o' charge!"

A murmuring sound of approval went up from the listeners. But all eyes were glued on the figure of McGee, whom they knew full well held their destinies in the hollow of his hand.

"Thet all?" demanded the giant, grimly.

"No, not quite, McGee," replied Daddy Mixer, hastily and pathetically. "He sez as how he wants to develop this country into a lumber region, and must have the help of the McGees. So he promises to pay wages as high as any in the State, and give full work every day in the year to every man or boy willing to enter his employ. And he winds up by saying he's gwine to come down here right soon hisself, to meet you-all, and fix up things just to suit everybody!"

Some one started to shout. It was an unfortunate move, for instantly the black look on the heavy face of McGee grew more gloomy. He raised his hand.

"Stop thet!" he roared, furiously. "Yuh pore fools, d'ye believe all this lyin' stuff thet Doc. Lancing has writ, jest tuh pull the wool over our eyes? It cain't be did! He's sure got sum slick trick up his sleeve. These younkers hes been sent down tuh find out all 'bout us; an' the sojers'll be along on ther heels tuh clar us out! I ain't gwine tuh take up wid no sech trash as thet. We gotter show Doc. Lancing we don't keer a mite foh his white flag. This hyah's his boy. Now we gat him weuns is bound tuh send him away wid the nicest coat o' tar an' feathers yuh ever heard tell on. That's my answer tuh Doc. Lancing, an' it goes, yuh hyah, men!"

Larry uttered a loud groan; and it seemed as though others among the listeners felt as down-spirited as did the Northern lad, to judge from the sighs around.

But right then and there, in the midst of all the tense excitement, there suddenly rang out a shot; followed by a scream from the lips of Tony McGee, who was seen darting forward to where a fluttering object lay struggling on the ground.

CHAPTER XXIII

THE "WINGED MESSENGER

"Oh! what was that? Who shot?" cried Larry, clutching his chum by the arm.

Phil pointed to a small boy who was trying to sneak away, carrying an old musket about half again as long as himself. He had possibly taken advantage of the excitement to steal his elder brother's gun; and casting about for some object upon which to exercise his ambitious marksmanship, had sighted a hovering bird, which had instantly fallen to his fire.

"But what makes Tony act like that?" demanded Larry.

Phil had divined the wonderful truth, even as his chum made his inquiry.

"It must have been one of his homing pigeons!" he exclaimed; "perhaps the one that he expected to bring him news from up-river way, about the girl in the hospital!"

"Oh! I wonder could that be so?" ejaculated Larry; and the two of them stood there, watching and waiting for they hardly knew what, only that into Phil's heart there seemed to have suddenly leaped a new and wild hope.

They saw Tony lift the little feathered messenger, and stroke its feathers, as he looked angrily around for the guilty youngster, who was already hiding behind one of the shanties.

"Look and see if it has a message from Tom Badger!" called Phil, himself quivering with eagerness and suspense.

Tony evidently had not thought of this at first, in his anger at having one of his precious pets slaughtered so ruthlessly. He sent a quick comprehending look toward his new chums, and instantly turned his attention again to the pigeon.

Immediately Phil saw him draw some small object from the bundle of crumpled feathers, which he began to unroll with great haste.

"It's a note from above," declared Phil, talking to himself, though Larry was listening with both ears to what he said. "The message has come, and just in the nick of time to save us from a mighty unpleasant experience. I hope it holds good news for Tony and his mother."

"It does—it must, Phil!" cried Larry. "Just look at Tony dancing around, would you? Oh! he's read something that's taken his voice away, you know! He can't even say anything; but see how his face talks! Phil, what d'ye think it can be?"

"Good news must mean the operation has taken place, and that it has been a success!" replied his chum, trying to master the tremor in his own voice, and hardly succeeding very well. "And can't you see just what that must mean for us, Larry, old fellow? Bring it here, Tony! Let us see what you have found!" and he beckoned to the boy while saying this.

But Tony made first of all for his mother, who was standing

there with clasped hands, in an agony betwixt doubt and hope. No sooner though, had her eager eyes devoured the contents of the tiny paper, than she fell to sobbing hysterically; but every one could see that it was joy and not grief that had caused this flow of tears from an overcharged heart.

She started toward McGee, holding out the bit of thin paper appealingly. McGee had been observing these several happenings with the same dark scowl on his brow; but he seemed to understand that news had come from the child who was so dear to him on account of her infirmity.

"Give hit tuh Daddy, an' let hin read hit!" he spoke up, as though even in that supreme moment something of the old doubt concerning his family remained.

Gladly did the woman turn to the shambling old man who came forward again. And as he bent over the tiny scrap of paper, as though endeavoring to make out what the writing on it meant, every sound ceased until the silence of death seemed to hover over that scene.

"Read hit out loud, Daddy!" commanded McGee, himself hardly able to restrain his own impatience.

"Operation a complete success! Child will soon see as well as any one! Shall bring her home myself tomorrow, and restore her to a mother's arms.

"DOCTOR GIDEON LANCING!"

Hardly had the last word been uttered than it seemed as though a tempest had suddenly descended upon that quiet little settlement in the midst of the cypress swamps. Every throat joined in the terrific shout that burst forth. Women threw their arms around one another; while rough men went about shaking hands, and wiping suspicious moisture from their sun-burned cheeks.

Phil and Larry whooped with the rest.

"It's all right, Larry!" cried the former, as he wrung his chum's hand with the vehemence of enthusiastic youth. "That's the last straw that breaks the camel's back! Even a McGee can't hold out against that evidence of friendship! Hurrah for my dad; and hurrah for us! But I say, Larry, it's lucky that poor little pigeon found its way home when it did, or we might have been turned into birds ourselves."

Even Larry could afford to laugh now at the heretofore gruesome outlook. As for Tony, he acted like one possessed; for he ran from his mother to his new chums, and back again; still gripping the lifeless form of the little winged messenger, as though he hardly knew what he was doing.

McGee had gone over to his wife, and taken her in his arms. The glorious news from above had done more to break down his iron nature than all other things combined; nor was Phil very much amazed to see how tenderly he soothed the mother of his children.

Then the big man strode over toward the spot where they stood; while every one watched curiously to see what he would do, for never yet had a man of them ever seen the mighty McGee bend the knee to any one.

"Gimme yuh hand, younker," he said, humbly enough. "I war all wrong, an' I admits hit right now an' hyah. Yuh dad he's jest a trump; an' w'en he kims tuh weuns' camp, thar ain't gwine tuh be a king welcomed more heartily'n he'll be. An' Tony boy, don't yuh do nawthin' tuh thet chile as shooted yuh bird, d'ye hyah? Ef 'twa'nt foh thet, jest see wot I'd a-done tuh the son o' the man as hes brought light tuh the blessed eyes o' our leetle Madge."

Again the shouts broke out. The entire settlement was mad with joy. Women got together and talked of the wonderful things that were going to come to pass when this benefactor fulfilled his promises, and their homes became a positive fact, with their men working every day at big wages, and a new life possessing the entire community.

Relieved from a terrible strain Phil and Larry began to take an interest in the many things connected with the squatter settlement. McGee, having thrown off his gloomy condition in the light of the happy news, showed that he was a keensighted man. He talked business with Phil in a way that quite pleased the boy; who felt positive that his father would find in this leading spirit of the swamp country just the able lieutenant he wanted, in order to make a big success of the new undertaking.

Of course the motor boat was soon brought down from its station above. Tony and his father accompanied the two voyagers up to get it; and McGee manifested considerable interest in the working of the smart little craft.

And then when on the third day there arrived a boat containing half a dozen persons, imagine the great joy when that good mother folded to her heart the form of the little child she had sent from her side with such great misgivings.

Of course Phil pounced on his father, the genial physician whose name as an oculist had long since become famous throughout the East. And as rapidly as he could, ably assisted by Larry, he poured out the wonderful story of their cruise, which had been brought to such a dramatic conclusion.

McGee was not long in welcoming Doctor Lancing, and in a day the two men seemed to understand each other thoroughly. Plans for the future were soon under way; and after several days spent among his neighbors, as the doctor termed those who were no longer squatters, since each family owned a tract of land besides that upon which their cabin was built, he again turned his face toward the north.

It might be well to say right here that things began to boom from that day; and at present the community where McGee still holds sway is a prosperous town, with happy homes, in which the comforts of life may be found, as well as a few of the luxuries. Little Madge did positively recover her sight, the bandages being removed before the departure of the great oculist.

Tony went down with Phil and Larry to the gulf, and spent a couple of months in their company that he would never forget. Later on he was given a chance to attend school, and one dream of his mother's heart was realized.

And Larry, too, learned many a useful lesson during that time, which would be apt to help him climb the ladder as an ambitious Boy Scout, once he found himself back in his home city.

Pete had turned up before they left for the gulf; and being supplied with more funds by Doctor Lancing kept on his way. Later on they heard from him in Mobile, where his family had joined him; and neither of the two Dixie Chums ever found reason to regret that they had helped him evade the "dawgs" of the vindictive Southern sheriff.

THE END

Choose from Thousands of 1stWorldLibrary Classics By

A. M. Barnard
Ada Leverson
Adolphus William Ward
Aesop
Agatha Christie
Alexander Aaronsohn
Alexander Kielland
Alexandre Dumas
Alfred Gatty
Alfred Ollivant
Alice Duer Miller
Alice Turner Curtis
Alice Dunbar
Allen Chapman
Alleyne Ireland
Ambrose Bierce
Amelia E. Barr
Amory H. Bradford
Andrew Lang
Andrew McFarland Davis
Andy Adams
Angela Brazil
Anna Alice Chapin
Anna Sewell
Annie Besant
Annie Hamilton Donnell
Annie Payson Call
Annie Roe Carr
Annonaymous
Anton Chekhov
Archibald Lee Fletcher
Arnold Bennett
Arthur C. Benson
Arthur Conan Doyle
Arthur M. Winfield
Arthur Ransome
Arthur Schnitzler
Arthur Train
Atticus
B.H. Baden-Powell
B. M. Bower
B. C. Chatterjee
Baroness Emmuska Orczy
Baroness Orczy
Basil King
Bayard Taylor
Ben Macomber
Bertha Muzzy Bower
Bjornstjerne Bjornson

Booth Tarkington
Boyd Cable
Bram Stoker
C. Collodi
C. E. Orr
C. M. Ingleby
Carolyn Wells
Catherine Parr Traill
Charles A. Eastman
Charles Amory Beach
Charles Dickens
Charles Dudley Warner
Charles Farrar Browne
Charles Ives
Charles Kingsley
Charles Klein
Charles Hanson Towne
Charles Lathrop Pack
Charles Romyn Dake
Charles Whibley
Charles Willing Beale
Charlotte M. Braeme
Charlotte M. Yonge
Charlotte Perkins Stetson
Clair W. Hayes
Clarence Day Jr.
Clarence E. Mulford
Clemence Housman
Confucius
Coningsby Dawson
Cornelis DeWitt Wilcox
Cyril Burleigh
D. H. Lawrence
Daniel Defoe
David Garnett
Dinah Craik
Don Carlos Janes
Donald Keyhoe
Dorothy Kilner
Dougan Clark
Douglas Fairbanks
E. Nesbit
E. P. Roe
E. Phillips Oppenheim
E. S. Brooks
Earl Barnes
Edgar Rice Burroughs
Edith Van Dyne
Edith Wharton

Edward Everett Hale
Edward J. O'Biren
Edward S. Ellis
Edwin L. Arnold
Eleanor Atkins
Eleanor Hallowell Abbott
Eliot Gregory
Elizabeth Gaskell
Elizabeth McCracken
Elizabeth Von Arnim
Ellem Key
Emerson Hough
Emilie F. Carlen
Emily Bronte
Emily Dickinson
Enid Bagnold
Enilor Macartney Lane
Erasmus W. Jones
Ernie Howard Pie
Ethel May Dell
Ethel Turner
Ethel Watts Mumford
Eugene Sue
Eugenie Foa
Eugene Wood
Eustace Hale Ball
Evelyn Everett-green
Everard Cotes
F. H. Cheley
F. J. Cross
F. Marion Crawford
Fannie E. Newberry
Federick Austin Ogg
Ferdinand Ossendowski
Fergus Hume
Florence A. Kilpatrick
Fremont B. Deering
Francis Bacon
Francis Darwin
Frances Hodgson Burnett
Frances Parkinson Keyes
Frank Gee Patchin
Frank Harris
Frank Jewett Mather
Frank L. Packard
Frank V. Webster
Frederic Stewart Isham
Frederick Trevor Hill
Frederick Winslow Taylor

Friedrich Kerst
Friedrich Nietzsche
Fyodor Dostoyevsky
G.A. Henty
G.K. Chesterton
Gabrielle E. Jackson
Garrett P. Serviss
Gaston Leroux
George A. Warren
George Ade
Geroge Bernard Shaw
George Cary Eggleston
George Durston
George Ebers
George Eliot
George Gissing
George MacDonald
George Meredith
George Orwell
George Sylvester Viereck
George Tucker
George W. Cable
George Wharton James
Gertrude Atherton
Gordon Casserly
Grace E. King
Grace Gallatin
Grace Greenwood
Grant Allen
Guillermo A. Sherwell
Gulielma Zollinger
Gustav Flaubert
H. A. Cody
H. B. Irving
H. C. Bailey
H. G. Wells
H. H. Munro
H. Irving Hancock
H. R. Naylor
H. Rider Haggard
H. W. C. Davis
Haldeman Julius
Hall Caine
Hamilton Wright Mabie
Hans Christian Andersen
Harold Avery
Harold McGrath
Harriet Beecher Stowe
Harry Castlemon
Harry Coghill
Harry Houidini

Hayden Carruth
Helent Hunt Jackson
Helen Nicolay
Hendrik Conscience
Hendy David Thoreau
Henri Barbusse
Henrik Ibsen
Henry Adams
Henry Ford
Henry Frost
Henry James
Henry Jones Ford
Henry Seton Merriman
Henry W Longfellow
Herbert A. Giles
Herbert Carter
Herbert N. Casson
Herman Hesse
Hildegard G. Frey
Homer
Honore De Balzac
Horace B. Day
Horace Walpole
Horatio Alger Jr.
Howard Pyle
Howard R. Garis
Hugh Lofting
Hugh Walpole
Humphry Ward
Ian Maclaren
Inez Haynes Gillmore
Irving Bacheller
Isabel Cecilia Williams
Isabel Hornibrook
Israel Abrahams
Ivan Turgenev
J. G.Austin
J. Henri Fabre
J. M. Barrie
J. M. Walsh
J. Macdonald Oxley
J. R. Miller
J. S. Fletcher
J. S. Knowles
J. Storer Clouston
J. W. Duffield
Jack London
Jacob Abbott
James Allen
James Andrews
James Baldwin

James Branch Cabell
James DeMille
James Joyce
James Lane Allen
James Lane Allen
James Oliver Curwood
James Oppenheim
James Otis
James R. Driscoll
Jane Abbott
Jane Austen
Jane L. Stewart
Janet Aldridge
Jens Peter Jacobsen
Jerome K. Jerome
Jessie Graham Flower
John Buchan
John Burroughs
John Cournos
John F. Kennedy
John Gay
John Glasworthy
John Habberton
John Joy Bell
John Kendrick Bangs
John Milton
John Philip Sousa
John Taintor Foote
Jonas Lauritz Idemil Lie
Jonathan Swift
Joseph A. Altsheler
Joseph Carey
Joseph Conrad
Joseph E. Badger Jr
Joseph Hergesheimer
Joseph Jacobs
Jules Vernes
Julian Hawthrone
Julie A Lippmann
Justin Huntly McCarthy
Kakuzo Okakura
Karle Wilson Baker
Kate Chopin
Kenneth Grahame
Kenneth McGaffey
Kate Langley Bosher
Kate Langley Bosher
Katherine Cecil Thurston
Katherine Stokes
L. A. Abbot
L. T. Meade

L. Frank Baum
Latta Griswold
Laura Dent Crane
Laura Lee Hope
Laurence Housman
Lawrence Beasley
Leo Tolstoy
Leonid Andreyev
Lewis Carroll
Lewis Sperry Chafer
Lilian Bell
Lloyd Osbourne
Louis Hughes
Louis Joseph Vance
Louis Tracy
Louisa May Alcott
Lucy Fitch Perkins
Lucy Maud Montgomery
Luther Benson
Lydia Miller Middleton
Lyndon Orr
M. Corvus
M. H. Adams
Margaret E. Sangster
Margret Howth
Margaret Vandercook
Margaret W. Hungerford
Margret Penrose
Maria Edgeworth
Maria Thompson Daviess
Mariano Azuela
Marion Polk Angellotti
Mark Overton
Mark Twain
Mary Austin
Mary Catherine Crowley
Mary Cole
Mary Hastings Bradley
Mary Roberts Rinehart
Mary Rowlandson
M. Wollstonecraft Shelley
Maud Lindsay
Max Beerbohm
Myra Kelly
Nathaniel Hawthrone
Nicolo Machiavelli
O. F. Walton
Oscar Wilde
Owen Johnson
P.G. Wodehouse
Paul and Mabel Thorne

Paul G. Tomlinson
Paul Severing
Percy Brebner
Percy Keese Fitzhugh
Peter B. Kyne
Plato
Quincy Allen
R. Derby Holmes
R. L. Stevenson
R. S. Ball
Rabindranath Tagore
Rahul Alvares
Ralph Bonehill
Ralph Henry Barbour
Ralph Victor
Ralph Waldo Emmerson
Rene Descartes
Ray Cummings
Rex Beach
Rex E. Beach
Richard Harding Davis
Richard Jefferies
Richard Le Gallienne
Robert Barr
Robert Frost
Robert Gordon Anderson
Robert L. Drake
Robert Lansing
Robert Lynd
Robert Michael Ballantyne
Robert W. Chambers
Rosa Nouchette Carey
Rudyard Kipling
Saint Augustine
Samuel B. Allison
Samuel Hopkins Adams
Sarah Bernhardt
Sarah C. Hallowell
Selma Lagerlof
Sherwood Anderson
Sigmund Freud
Standish O'Grady
Stanley Weyman
Stella Benson
Stella M. Francis
Stephen Crane
Stewart Edward White
Stijn Streuvels
Swami Abhedananda
Swami Parmananda
T. S. Ackland

T. S. Arthur
The Princess Der Ling
Thomas A. Janvier
Thomas A Kempis
Thomas Anderton
Thomas Bailey Aldrich
Thomas Bulfinch
Thomas De Quincey
Thomas Dixon
Thomas H. Huxley
Thomas Hardy
Thomas More
Thornton W. Burgess
U. S. Grant
Upton Sinclair
Valentine Williams
Various Authors
Vaughan Kester
Victor Appleton
Victor G. Durham
Victoria Cross
Virginia Woolf
Wadsworth Camp
Walter Camp
Walter Scott
Washington Irving
Wilbur Lawton
Wilkie Collins
Willa Cather
Willard F. Baker
William Dean Howells
William le Queux
W. Makepeace Thackeray
William W. Walter
William Shakespeare
Winston Churchill
Yei Theodora Ozaki
Yogi Ramacharaka
Young E. Allison
Zane Grey